Walking
with
Nehemiah

Joseph W. Daniels Jr.

Walking
with
Nehemiah

Your Community
Is Your Congregation

Abingdon Press
Nashville

WALKING WITH NEHEMIAH:
YOUR COMMUNITY IS YOUR CONGREGATION

Copyright © 2014 by Abingdon Press

All rights reserved.

This book is printed on acid-free paper.

Library of Congress Cataloging-in-Publication Data

Daniels, Joseph W.
  Walking with Nehemiah : your community is your congregation / Joseph W. Daniels, Jr.
    pages cm
  Includes bibliographical references.
  ISBN 978-1-4267-8193-3 (binding: pbk., adhesive perfect binding : alk. paper)
1. Mission of the church. 2. Church work. 3. Evangelistic work. 4. Communities—Religious aspects—Christianity. 5. Neighborhoods. 6. Bible. Nehemiah—Criticism, interpretation, etc. I. Title.
  BV601.8.D36 2014
  269'.2—dc23

                                                                          2014021467

Disclaimer: Some names and details have been changed to protect the identity of persons. Other persons have given the author permission for use of their story.

14 15 16 17 18 19 20 21 22 23—10 9 8 7 6 5 4 3 2 1

MANUFACTURED IN THE UNITED STATES OF AMERICA

Contents

Acknowledgments   vii

Introduction   xi

Step 1: Feel Your Heart Break   1

Step 2: Pray for Next Steps   15

Step 3: Give It Your All   29

Step 4: Take the Risk   39

Step 5: Inspect Your Mission Field   49

Step 6: Gain Commitment   63

Step 7: Get to Work   75

Step 8: Expect Opposition   89

Step 9: Build Momentum   101

Appendix: Relational 1:1 Campaign Example   115

Acknowledgments

I am so grateful to God through my Lord and Savior, Jesus Christ, that this book can be shared with those seeking to build the kingdom of God. This book has come to pass solely because of the grace of God; God's grace that has been unspeakably and unimaginably good to me.

Within this grace continues to be the timeless love, loyal presence, surreal sacrifice, and constant, abiding support of my wife of twenty-nine years, Madelyn Daniels. When I met Madelyn thirty-four years ago, my best man and childhood friend, Mark Bright, told me I "lucked out." Well, he was so right. But I didn't just "luck out"; I have discovered that God simply drew me into a deep, intimate relationship with my best friend that among many things, makes it possible to do ministry. Madelyn's quiet, confident companionship creates the atmosphere for me to be able to do what God calls me to do. For that and many things, I am eternally grateful!

Within this grace is the overwhelming love and radiant joy of my young adult children, Joia and Joey. God has blessed me with the best daughter and son in the world. They love me in spite of me and inspire me in ways they can't even imagine. I give God thanks!

Within this grace is the gracious loving, caring, embracing, and encouraging spirit of Emory United Methodist Church in Washington, DC, affectionately known as "The Emory Fellowship." This amazing church full of amazing people from all parts of the world continues to mold and shape me in pastoral ministry, even after twenty-two years together. Through relevant, enthusiastic, authentic, and loving ministry, we seek to meet tangible needs in a very diverse community and inspire people to become followers and learners of Jesus Christ. For the Fellowship, I give God praise! For Troy Watson, our executive director, and Carolyn Anderson, our director of congregational life, who lead us in phenomenal ways; for Ann London, our certified lay minister, and Raphael Koikoi, our associate pastor, who make it happen behind the scenes; for Hazel Broadnax, the president of our nonprofit, the Emory Beacon of Light, Inc., and Alisa Molyneaux, the Beacon of Light's executive director, who lead our connection to the community; and for Loraine Trotter-Wrenn, the chair of our lead team; Dearl Wrenn, our lay leader; and all the leaders of Emory, I simply and sincerely say, "Thank you!"

Within this grace is found the selfless sharing, constant commitment, and deep devotion of Christine Shinn Latona, who gave of her precious time, energy, wisdom, and intellect to work with me on this production from beginning to end and make key contributions to this effort. Christie is an unbelievable gift to God's church, a blessing to so many leaders, pastors, churches, and annual conferences across the country and world. I'm humbled to be counted in the number. Bless the Lord!

And within this grace are the wonderful people of the Baltimore-Washington Conference of The United Methodist Church led by Bishop Marcus Matthews—particularly the pastors and laity of the powerful, profound, and prophetic Greater Washington District with whom I walk with Nehemiah as district superintendent and a pastor. We are truly seeking to develop our communities as our congregations in simple, yet creative and innovative ways. To God be the glory for a first class district staff: Christie Latona, our regional strategist, and Olivia Gross, our district administrator. To God be the glory for the great things God is doing!

I pray that this book is a blessing to the Kingdom builders who read it. Amen!

Introduction

One of the greatest challenges to the church in the twenty-first century is its lack of connection to its community. Far too many churches today have become drive-in, spiritual social clubs and not the agents of community vitality and life transformation they used to be. As a result, communities are suffering, churches are dying, and far too many people are searching for hope in all the wrong places.

Imprinted in my mind are many of the stories that my mom speaks of with regards to the church and the community where she grew up in Pittsburgh, Pennsylvania. Though my grandmother was Pentecostal and my grandfather unchurched, my mother and her siblings closest to her age went to the Presbyterian church in the neighborhood. When I asked my mom why this was, she said it was the result of the pastor and the people of that church actively reaching out to parents and children, seeking to engage children in positive activities that built character, integrity, and the soul.

Now at eighty-two years of age, she still speaks glowingly of how that church taught kids to read, helped teenagers find jobs, and sent young people to camp so they could learn new things and see that the world was bigger than their neighborhood. She still speaks of how the church helped people find scant opportunities to go to college and how many in the neighborhood got married in that church and moved on to prosperous and productive lives, even in the midst of the challenges of society. That church had such a profound impact on my mother's life that she still talks about trying to return to visit the church and spend time with people she still knows in the community, even though she's resided away from Pittsburgh most of her life.

Today, that church is struggling to stay alive, let alone thrive. Many of the behaviors that caused such impact years ago are no longer creating the positive influence of days gone by. The passion of the congregation to be the center of community life, ensuring that the community around it was everything that God in his word promised it could be, is waning. As a result, the congregation and community are just a remnant of what they used to be.

Unfortunately, this is the reality of a vast majority of churches today. Even megachurches that have grown by leaps and bounds often struggle with a drive-in, drive-out attitude that doesn't bother to engage the very people around them. I remember speaking to a dear friend of mine who was a leader in a five-thousand-member congregation who, when I complimented him and his church for the great things they were doing, said to me that "the reality of it, Joe, is that only 125 people here actually do the ministry. If they left, we'd be in big trouble. Most of the people here are just coming or going and really don't connect."

I'm afraid that if the patterns described above continue, the

church in America will be in serious trouble. And the communities surrounding our gathered fellowships will be in trouble just
the same. While the gospel is clear that the gates of hell will not
prevail against the church, the organized church's influence among
the masses is struggling. The signs are already there. Fewer than
20 percent of Americans worship in any community of faith in
any weekend. (This statistic has been replicated in two indepen-
dent studies, both cited here: Rebecca Barnes and Lindy Lowry,
"7 Startling Facts: An Up Close Look at Church Attendance
in America," Church Leaders, http://www.churchleaders.com
/pastors/pastor-articles/139575-7-startling-facts-an-up-close
-look-at-church-attendance-in-america.html.) And too many
neighborhoods—rural, suburban, and urban—show signs of
moral, ethical, social, and economic decay. Our society will
crumble if the people of God do not return to serious community
engagement informed by a return to covenantal relationship with
God and others, as was found in the book of Nehemiah, Acts 2,
and anywhere Jesus went.

John Wesley, the founder of Methodism, famously stated,
"The world is my parish." His statement reminds us that we have a
fabulous opportunity to interact, engage, build relationships, and
make disciples with the people living and working in the communities surrounding us. We must view the community as our
congregation. We must see the corner store and its owner, Ms.
Campbell, as our classroom and treat Ms. Campbell as a cher-
ished member, whether she belongs to our church or not. We
must see Mr. Taylor, the principal, and his elementary school as
an extension campus. We must persuade the mayor of our town,
Ms. Kelley, to be a collaborative partner in the rebuilding of broken parts of our neighborhood.

In spite of evidence to the contrary, I believe that we are at a moment where if we return to our biblical roots of community engagement and covenantal relationship, we will reclaim the church's rightful place as the center for life and community transformation. The challenges are not insurmountable.

The challenge for most people is building authentic relationships that are mutually beneficial—relationships that build community vitality. It isn't that congregations don't know that they are supposed to be outwardly focused. There is conversation in many churches about reaching out to the community. In fact, most congregations have some type of outreach ministry. There are many congregations bustling with food pantries, soup kitchens, clothes closets, and other great services that help people. The problem is that if we ask the people engaged in these serving ministries the names of those they are serving, where they live, what's going on in their lives, why they are hungry, and what is the deeper need in order for them to reach God's dream for their lives and their community—the answer for most is, "I don't know." We are often doing ministry for people, but not with people. Many of us are doing "caring" ministry, but are we engaged in "transformational" ministry? Jesus always knew the identity of those he touched. Even if he didn't know everyone by name, he knew the root cause of their human condition; he was always ready to change someone's life for the better, and he was positioned to help them see the power of being in a deep, abiding relationship with him.

People need to learn how to forge new relationships that can be cultivated in a way that brings positive community change. It's amazing in this social media–crazed world how difficult it is for many people to have a simple conversation with someone else. Particularly someone else they don't know very well. I was surprised in a recent relational training with handpicked leaders in our church how difficult it was for many of them to even fathom setting up a one-on-one conversation with someone they didn't know well. The fear of speaking up and just talking with someone was visible and prevalent. As we become more dependent on texting, tweeting, and instant messaging, it seems as if we need to regain the art of having deep conversations with one another that build authentic relationships—the foundation of strong community ties.

A friend of mine grew up in an immigrant neighborhood where everyone knew each other. He tells of the reality that not only did he and others in his community know their next-door neighbors, but also they knew the neighbors at the end of the block. And when he said he and others knew them, it was more than just what car they drove and what their name was. They knew them because they were in constant contact. They talked with neighbors, went to school with neighbors, ate with them, played with them, borrowed pantry items from them, and knew when things were going well or not going well with them.

There was also great concern for those who were vulnerable and defenseless in this community. If one family had means and someone else didn't, the family that had an abundance shared. If someone needed help and others could provide it, others offered help. If someone simply needed others to be present, the presence of others was often enough to get them through whatever crisis was going on in his or her life. If the local school needed more books or more volunteers, the community organized to respond to the need. If the church needed a new boiler, the neighborhood began collecting money. If children began to go astray, Mr. Joe or Ms. Susie up the street instantly and rapidly got them back in line and then told their parents, who then gave another round of discipline. This is what community looks like when people in the community know and invest in one another. This is what community looks like in Acts 2. This is what community can look like if we decide we will invest in relationships with those in our community like Nehemiah did.

Displaced from his community because of captivity, Nehemiah discovers a passion within himself to rebuild the community he once knew in Jerusalem. Inspired by the grace of God, doors opened for him to reengage his people in community restoration. By no means was the task easy; in fact, without God, it was impossible. Yet the process God led Nehemiah through gives us great insight into how we can partner with God and others to transform community and bring hope to those who are vulnerable and defenseless.

Participate in this walk with Nehemiah and discover what people God is asking you to encourage, what walls God is calling you to repair, what ministry God might be calling you to lead or do, and where. By finding your own answers to the following questions, you will be able to build meaningful relationships and participate in a movement of restoration in your community that you and your congregation never thought possible.

Step 1: Feel your heart break. It isn't until you know for whom or what your heart breaks that God can reveal where in the community and with whom your ministry needs to be done. This brokenheartedness isn't just the stuff of love songs; it is what lifelong missions are made of. (Nehemiah 1:1-4)

Step 2: Pray for next steps. If you sincerely pray, God will create a way for you to help the very people and situations that break your heart. Nehemiah shows us how to sincerely pray: by recognizing God as the Lord of our lives, by understanding that God keeps his covenant with us, and by confessing our sins and the sins of others. (Nehemiah 1:5-11)

Step 3: Give it your all. You cannot be fully engaged without giving it your all. You cannot help people rebuild lives or community with a lukewarm or sloppy effort. At some point God's call for you to deal with your heartbreak and engage yourself in transformative work is going to require that you be passionately "all-in." (Nehemiah 1:10-11)

Step 4: Take the risk. If you risk positioning yourself for his purposes and use your position for his purposes, God will get you all you need to change lives and communities for the better. You don't have to be in a position of privilege in order to have your position count. Sometimes we don't think our position is significant. Yet when we surrender our agenda to God's agenda, God can use our position to turn things around for the better. (Nehemiah 2:1-9)

Step 5: Inspect your mission field. Too often we end up doing ministry for people instead of with people. This happens because of two things: we see an "us" and "them" divide, and we identify a need based on statistics or what we think needs to be done, instead of building relationships with those in the community and letting them tell us what they will partner with us to accomplish. If, like Nehemiah, you walk before you talk, then when you talk, people will walk with you. (Nehemiah 2:11-16)

Step 6: Gain commitment. When our action is rooted in who our hearts break for, when we pray for God's next steps, when we're all-in, take risks, and take the time to inspect our mission field, we soon discover that gaining the commitment of others is possible and necessary. This is particularly true when we are prayerful and strategic about it. Before Nehemiah surveyed the situation, he saw himself as one of the community. This enabled him to speak the truth and summon the people to rise up. (Nehemiah 2:17-18)

Step 7: Get to work. Any community engagement effort requires strong organization. People need to know what their assignments are and what is expected of them. Additionally, folks need to learn how to stay in their lane while supporting the common good. (Nehemiah 3)

Step 8: Expect opposition. Whenever a group of people commits itself to the common good—and are fully engaged in bringing hope to the vulnerable and defenseless—you can expect that some people will ridicule and others will not participate. It is critical to keep your attention on those who are engaged and not be distracted by others. (Nehemiah 2:19; 3:5, 4:1-9; 6:1-3)

Step 9: Build momentum. To get to the finish line you've got to become friends with "Big Mo." Big Mo, in case you haven't met him or her, is momentum. If you want to experience victory, you had better pay attention to momentum and do all you can to build it from the start of your heartbreak to its resolution. (Nehemiah 4:13-15; 6:1-4, 9, 15)

Journey with Nehemiah and discover who God is asking you to encourage, what walls God is calling you to repair, what ministry God might be calling you to lead, and where. It is my prayer that you will find inspiration and practical tools for engaging with your community in ways that help you, your congregation, and your community become whole.

Step 1

Feel Your Heart Break

I t isn't until you know for whom or what your heart breaks
that God can reveal where in the community and with
whom your ministry needs to be done. This brokenheartedness isn't just the stuff of love songs; it is what lifelong missions
are made of.

These are the words of Nehemiah, Hacaliah's son.
In the month of Kislev, in the twentieth year, while I was in the fortress
city of Susa, Hanani, one of my brothers, came with some other men
from Judah. I asked them about the Jews who had escaped and survived
the captivity, and about Jerusalem.
They told me, "Those in the province who survived the captivity are in
great trouble and shame! The wall around Jerusalem is broken down,
and its gates have been destroyed by fire!"
When I heard this news, I sat down and wept. I mourned for days, fast-
ing and praying before the God of heaven.
Nehemiah 1:1-4

1

Who Does Your Heart Break For?

That's a good question. That's a deep question. That's a real soul-searching question. When somebody asks it of me, I find that my heart has really been broken for the last thirty-three years, since I was a sophomore in college. No, not over my high school prom date who was "fine as frog hair" as one of my colleagues in ministry says; a "fox" as we used to say in those days—a woman I had a "thing" for, but who then dropped me after my freshman year in college following some of my own foolishness. But ironically my heart broke over the church; in particular, churches so self-centered and disconnected from what was really happening in people's lives and communities that they were completely out of touch—blind and ignorant to the power of Jesus to resurrect broken lives, situations, and neighborhoods.

I grew up in a church like that. It was a church that wouldn't even grant me, then a college student, and another childhood friend of mine permission to start and conduct a Bible study that we and many other young people in the community sorely needed. We were trying to deal with the challenges of following Jesus while being daily impacted by peer pressure, drug abuse, sexual enticements, family strife, street violence, "-isms," and other conflicts poised to destroy us. We were seeking to find meaning in our lives. Yet our church, after our phenomenal youth leader Ruby Bentley died, suddenly stopped hearing our cries. I can still hear the administrative board chair's voice say to us, "No. You cannot do that here. Not in this church."

That *no*, broke my heart. Now, there were individual voices standing up and embracing us, and how we thank God for them. I don't know where we'd be without them. But when we needed

2

the collective institution to open a door to us, the church said no. And that *no* caused me to reach the tipping point that drove me away from church for a few years.

Thank God I had a Thursday night Bible study to go to in the living room of a friend's house. Thank God my best friend's uncle would later empower me to start with him an additional Wednesday night study in the basement of a neighborhood library. These two gatherings became church for me. They became my community. I was one of eleven people who would emerge from those studies experiencing a call to ordained ministry on my life. And when I finally stopped running from and rebelling against God's summons of me to serve as a pastor in God's church—some six years after hearing that word, *no*—I made a vow to God and myself that I would do all I could, in the name of Jesus, to not allow any congregation to which I was appointed fall into that trap of saying no to positive community-building possibilities. By God's grace, I would lead a church to not be so focused on our internal machinations that we are unable to help people from all walks of life in the community find wholeness in Jesus Christ—physically, emotionally, mentally, spiritually, relationally, and economically. I find that I've been working on that heartbreak ever since.

That's the short version of my heartbreak. It has propelled the rest of my life's work. But much more important in the here and now, whom does your heart break for?

Asking people to feel their heart break is not exactly the greatest beginning to any story, chapter, sermon, speech, or book. Certainly not in this violence-promoting, mixed martial arts–crazed, pleasure-seeking, football-concussed, and microwave-convenienced society we live in.

Truly, it is countercultural to ask people to feel their heartbreak, especially when people are spending tons of money and energy to escape pain or to identify their passion, joy, exuberance, bliss, or meaning in life.

Start a book with heartbreak? You have to be kidding me. How about beginning with an intriguing story, a humorous tale, an adventurous journey instead. Wouldn't that be better? Feel my heartbreak?

Ironically, the Latin root of the word *passion* means "to suffer." So, we can't find our passion in life without somehow embracing the corresponding pain. Furthermore, discovering our deep passions often links us to some sort of suffering event or circumstance, situations that can be frightening or not fun to experience. And while visiting these realities certainly is not our cup of tea or our soul's greatest desire, the fact of the matter is that you and I cannot find the deep meaning, purpose, plan, or vision for our lives until we identify that passion, until we feel our heartbreak.

When we begin reading the story of Nehemiah, we cannot get past the first four verses of the first chapter without having to confront heartbreak. Nehemiah's name means "the Lord has comforted." Yet when we look at the state he's in at the beginning of his story, we do not see someone whom the Lord is comforting. Nor do we see someone whom the Lord is using to comfort others in the midst of their trials. Rather we see a high-level Hebrew leader noble in character whose dream must have burst in the face of Babylonian exile. Nehemiah is a slave in Babylonian captivity hired to make sure one person, Artaxerxes, the king of Persia, is comforted beyond his kingly comfort.

Nehemiah is the king's cupbearer in the royal palace. The royal bartender, if you don't mind me saying. He's got what my wife calls a GGJ—a good government job—something folks in Wash-

4

ington, DC, are famous for saying. He's working for the president in the White House. His boss could have been the prime minister in Great Britain or His Excellency in many other countries. He's the butler of that day. Yes, he's serving the king wine, but he was the king's trusted assistant. He was the most trusted person in the king's court because kings cannot be nonchalant about who is serving them wine. People can poison your wine, you know!

But although Nehemiah is in the uncomfortable place of bondage, he grows comfortable. For a slave, he's living large and in charge. He's in the king's palace. He's not doing what he's been called to do, born to do, or named to do. But he's comfortable. A lot of folks that I run into, day after day, are in bondage, but they are comfortable. They are not living out what God created them to live out or what their parents sent them to school to live out, but they are comfortable. How many of us are not doing what we want to do or what God called us to do but are comfortable?

But one day, all of this changed for Nehemiah. And one day, it very well may change for you, too—especially if you're living life comfortably. Comfort is not about how much money you make or how big your house is or what kind of car you drive. Comfort is about being satisfied with the status quo, even when you know God is calling you to change it. If you are comfortable with the way things are, even when you know they should be different; if you've been called, let alone named, to comfort those who are afflicted but are ignoring it; if you are trying to maintain a comfort level that is inconsistent with God's plan for your life, God is going to knock on your door and disturb you. God is going to remind you that he didn't call you to be comfortable. He called you to comfort the disturbed. And if you're going to do his will in restoring broken lives and communities, you will have to let go of your comfort—even in captivity—and let God use you to get engaged in the lives of hurting souls needing to be restored!

God used Nehemiah's own brother, Hanani, to get Nehemiah's attention. It must be really something when your own family member comes to you with a message from God that unexpectedly hits you right between the eyes and shatters you at the depth of your soul. If you are like me, family members can come to us with a whole lot of stuff—and most of the time it is not a word from the Lord. In the words of the comedian "Huggy Lowdown," sometimes they come with "shiggity." But Hanani comes to get Nehemiah's attention. And he doesn't just come by himself. He comes with Nehemiah's boys from the hood. He comes with representatives from the Hebrew community in Babylon to share with Nehemiah some disturbing news.

Before they can open their mouths, Nehemiah asks them how things are back home. They say to him, "Well, bruh, you need to understand that things back home are not good. The folks who escaped captivity and eluded bondage—our peeps—are in great trouble and distress. The walls in Jerusalem are torn down and the gates are burned up. There is a political, social, economic, spiritual, and community mess."

As Nehemiah listens to this disturbing news, we can almost hear the crumbling sound of his heart breaking and see the devastation painted all over his face. A broken heart is more than us just being upset. When our hearts break, it changes our whole countenance, our whole attitude, the very way we live, move, and have our being. When Nehemiah's heart breaks, he sits down and weeps. He weeps for the Jewish remnant, his brothers and sisters in Jerusalem, who are in great trouble and disgrace because Jerusalem, his home, is in shambles from the Babylonian invasion.

His people are left vulnerable and defenseless against the evils of society.

To be left vulnerable and defenseless is no small order. The truth is that when your "walls" are destroyed and your "gates" are burned down—physically, emotionally, spiritually, financially, or relationally—you have nothing to defend yourself with. You become a target for being taken advantage of. You unjustly and unfairly and, at times, unfathomably suffer. There is nothing to protect an individual or community from the cold, callous, and cruel advances that often come from adversarial foes. You no longer have the ability to choose whom you let in or whom you keep out of your life. All of that is eradicated. And considering the fact that the people of Jerusalem were under siege, this was the people's daily reality.

And when Nehemiah hears this, his heart breaks. He sits down and weeps. And he doesn't just weep for a few minutes. We are told that he did so for days. Please understand that Nehemiah wasn't a crybaby, a weak man, or a chump. Nehemiah was a tough dude. He was a strong, courageous, risk-taking, bold kind of man. But when he hears the news, it shakes him so deeply that he sits down and weeps. For days!

What causes you to sit down and weep for days? Over whom does your soul mourn and grieve over for days on end?

This strife bothers Nehemiah such that it grips him, consumes him, won't let him go. You know you've got something going on within you that you've got to respond to when it grips you, wrestles with you, consumes you, disturbs you, troubles you, bothers you, stirs up agony in you, and refuses to let you go. It breaks his heart.

Whom does your heart break for? I can imagine Nehemiah

finds himself burdened with a heartsick responsibility that he can't shake. I can envision him finding himself handcuffed with a heartfelt calling to now comfort hurting families back home that are his own blood. Surely, he can't sleep much. He probably goes to bed at night thinking about it. He wakes up in the middle of the night thinking about it. He feels it with him as he rises in the morning. He mourns and grieves about it as he serves the king throughout the day.

Whom does your heart break for? What vulnerable or defenseless situation or circumstance in life causes you to grieve for days on end? Have you identified it yet? Whom do you sit down and weep in your spirit over? What in your life has you so burdened that if you don't respond to it, it's going to drive you crazy? Have you heard news that cuts you to the heart so deeply that you are shaken by it, consumed by it such that you have to trade in your life of comfort so that you can go do something about it?

Whom does your heart break for? What devastating situation is bothering you such that it's leading you to take some different and significant steps in your life to heal the pain and bring about change? Kids are shooting at other kids in schools across the country and across socioeconomic class structures. Does that bother you? Men of one particular race are subjected to mass incarceration such that there are almost five times more black men in jail than white males (see Bureau of Justice Statistics, "Number of State Prisoners Declined by Almost 3,000 during 2009; Federal Prison Population Increased by 6,800," June 23, 2010, http://www.bjs.gov/content/pub/press/pim09stpy09acpr.cfm). Does that trouble you? Children by the thousands are being abused, mistreated, and sex trafficked all over the world. Does that burden you? In the wealthiest country in the world, homelessness is rampant. Does that grieve you? Citizenship status is a political football while many immigrants who have been here for years and have families rooted here wake up daily with fears of deportation, never mind basic survival. Does that consume you? As people in power move special interest groups like pawns—granting some groups basic civil rights while stripping other groups of civil rights long fought for and earned—even though everyone deserves civil rights, does that unsettle you? Does anything break your heart to the point that you have to do something about it?

The way to discover your passion is to answer this question—whom does your heart break for? If you know whom your heart breaks for, you will know who you need to be in ministry with and where that ministry needs to take place. Your life will find meaning, purpose, and passion. If you do not answer the question "whom does my heart break for?" or even bother to pause to feel your heartbreak, you will miss out on knowing your function in the body of Christ at this point in your journey. Furthermore, you may wander aimlessly trying to figure out what God wants you to do to build the Kingdom. Too many people are wandering aimlessly when God wants us to find God and discover all of the greatness that God has in store for us—greatness often discovered in restoring broken lives and communities.

The renowned civil rights leader Martin Luther King Jr. once wrote, "If a man has not found something worth dying for, he is not fit to live."

Rick Warren says, "Other people are going to find healing in your wounds. Your greatest life messages and your most effective ministry will come out of your deepest hurts" (*The Purpose-Driven Life: What on Earth Am I Here For?*, [Grand Rapids: Zondervan, 2002], 275). You've got to discover what breaks your heart. When you do, lives and communities will change for the better. Hope will be restored to countless multitudes who are hopeless!

In Nehemiah, we see his most effective ministry birthed out of deep pain. His people are suffering and struggling, and he can't do anything about it. In the twinkling of an eye, Nehemiah discovers that slavery and exile are not the only things trapping him; what really has a hold on him is a summons by God to leave his comfortable confines of the king's court and engage with the troubled and shamed people in his community called Jerusalem, helping to improve their lives.

You and Your Congregation Can Do Something with Your Heartbreak

Nehemiah reminds me of two very ordinary guys in my congregation. One is a retired public service employee who grew up on meager means; the other is a former communications specialist who has lived in the United States for almost forty years. Both, however, in the midst of their comfort, found their hearts broken and their lives changed mightily after participating in a yearlong Bible study together at their church.

Through the study, and through authentic, transparent sharing with their fellow learners, the two heard a collective call to take the gospel to the street corner in their church's neighborhood. During the study, their hearts began breaking for the men they'd see almost every day on the corner; men who'd become vulnerable and defenseless due to demoralizing life events leading to alcohol and drug addiction, unemployment, homelessness, and despair.

These men had great familiarity with the neighborhood. One man's workplace was just a couple blocks away from the church, and the other man used to live in the neighborhood and still did much of his shopping there. And both of them yearned to support men—one of them having missed out on being nurtured and supported by men growing up; the other having been blessed by the presence of strong men in his life. Furthermore, each of them had negative experiences with alcohol in their own lives and felt compelled to go to one of the most notorious blocks in the neighborhood to see if God might open a door for them to transform broken lives.

The street they went to was known as "Crack Alley." Many men had given up on life, had squatted in the corner apartment buildings, and had begun destroying themselves on drugs that were plentiful from dealers lining the block. It was a corner of despair. But the two men in my congregation, having seen and touched despair in their own lives, prayed to be used by God to change the lives of those men on the block with alcohol and drug addiction.

It was far from an easy task. Getting men to come off the corner for a Sunday afternoon of soup and study at the church next door was much harder at first than they thought. Getting addicts to come out of their comfort zone is not the easiest thing to do. But after a period of prayer, asking God for an opportunity to minister to those their hearts broke for, suddenly one man came, and then another. Before they knew it, lives began to be impacted. And soon thereafter, the two men I know had their congregation engaging the heartbreak with them. An additional worship service was started. A ministry to the homeless began. Even a jobs ministry got off the ground. And every week persons with very little found a hot meal and warm hearts as a foundational place for them to get up on their feet.

Congregations who are doing vital ministry with their communities are filled with passionate, heartbroken people like these two men—Nehemiahs of today. When the desire to restore those who are vulnerable and defenseless is in the DNA of congregations, those congregations actually attract certain types of heartbroken people because of their particular vision and work in the community. There are churches across the country and world that have a reputation for ministry with the poor, for working with addicts, or for leading ministries of reconciliation. Their clear outreach and advocacy in these areas naturally draw people who are likewise heartbroken for these populations.

What about your church? For whom does your congregation's heart break?

Some churches come to a fresh vision because of people who discover whom their hearts break for and then are empowered to develop plans and ministries that rebuild specific walls. For example, I know of one woman, who, remembering the moments in her life when she was one paycheck from homelessness when supporting herself and her two young kids, discovered later in life that God was summoning her to work with her congregation to establish a transitional housing ministry. After being not far from homelessness herself, she and members of her church now ensure that families facing similar circumstances have a temporary roof over their head until they can find their own.

Another church in an affluent suburb of one city had a woman whose heart broke for the hungry people in her community. She began to organize monthly dinners, then expanded to a weekly pantry that involved more and more of the congregation. What began as a shared passion for feeding hungry people in their community has become a community-wide campaign to end hunger within the church's zip code. Amongst many things, the food pantry has sparked a fire to serve within the congregation and is shaping a long-term vision for the congregation's future. Members now proclaim: "We are all about feeding people."

How is your congregation helping people identify whom their hearts break for? At my church, we have discovered many different pathways that seem to help. We have seen people identify whom their hearts break for as a result of a church-wide campaign to engage in community and through sermon series seeking to help people identify passion. We've seen people discover whom their hearts break for through Disciple Bible study and other small-group settings. We've even seen people make this discovery through our class offerings called "Living on Purpose," intentionally designed to help congregants discover and embrace God's call on their lives. By offering an avenue of discovery at different congregational seasons, we have found a way to keep the fire stoked. In addition to helping people discover their spiritual giftedness and test-drive a ministry based on that giftedness, we are also starting to raise that question in our new members class.

How is your congregation organizing and equipping around the answers to these questions? It is essential that you have a plan and people in place to help shepherd newly found passions into constructive ministry. There is nothing quite so depressing as watching sparks fly and then get extinguished due to lack of oxygen or other external forces. Nothing is quite as disappointing as seeing multitudes of people never discover their passion, joy, or purpose in life.

Whom does your heart break for?

Personal: Whom does your heart break for? Does whom your

*"Remember the word that you gave to your servant Moses when you said,
'If you are unfaithful, I will scatter you among the peoples. But if you
return to me and keep my commandments by really doing them, then,
even though your outcasts live under distant skies, I will gather them
from there and bring them to the place that I have chosen as a dwelling
for my name.' They are your servants and your people. They are the ones
whom you have redeemed by your great power and your strong hand.
"LORD, let your ear be attentive to the prayer of your servant and to the
prayer of your servants who delight in honoring your name. Please give
success to your servant today and grant him favor in the presence of this
man!"
At that time, I was a cupbearer to the king.*

—Nehemiah 1:5-11

What Do You Need to Pray For?

I don't know about you, but for me, when I get heartbreaking
news, I go through multiple reactions. I get very quiet, become no-
ticeably isolated, and attempt to keep others from seeing my devastation. Numerous thoughts rush through my head; file cabinets of
past and current feelings flip forward to the forefront of my mind.

I think of the heartbreak. I feel the pain of the heartbreak. I
connect the heartbreak to previous pains like it. I wrestle. I worry.
I wonder if and when I'll overcome. I ponder whether I have the
strength to overcome. Can God really overcome troubles? Do I
have the patience to walk with God through it? Will the pain be
too great? Will it be too oppressive? How will it impact all of the
facets of my life? When heartbreaking news hits my doorstep, it's
not the most settled time for my mind, body, and soul.

16

But I'm not the only one who experiences heartbreak. We all do. And the question is, when we find ourselves at points like this in life, what's our next step?

One stretch of heartbreaking news devastated me in high school. A series of deaths of loved ones in my extended family had rocked me. An education scandal uncovering the fact that I'd been an intentional victim of racism and discrimination in my school shook me. Politics in athletics left my star basketball season my junior year unnoticed and unrecognized in postseason awards and accolades—in an unfair, unjust, and brutal way. Add to that the beginning of the unraveling of my parents' marriage and, needless to say, things were getting a little tough. In the words of one of my best friends at the time, "If it ain't one thing, it's another."

But I'll never forget a word of hope that my Uncle Pete gave me during this very difficult period in my life. There he was, hundreds of miles away, sending me a message that has undergirded me in powerful and profound ways since then. He said, "Joseph, it ain't how you fall, it's how you get back up." He was letting me know that we are all going to fall. Every now and then, we are all going to have heartbreaking news creep into our lives. But he was also encouraging me to see a bigger picture. A picture that revealed that although heartbreak is a fact of life, heartbreak does not have to define life. Our lives depend on how we get back up. And, the lives of others depend on how we get back up. If we get up, they can get up! Donny McClurkin, the popular gospel singer, put it this way: "A saint is just a sinner who fell down, . . . and got up."

Nehemiah chooses not to let the heartbreaking news that felled him keep him down. He decides to get back up. But it is how he gets back up that is important for us to understand so that

17

we too might rise up and rise above the heartbreak in ways that allow us to participate with God and others in doing something about the heartbreak. Yes, perhaps we can even change lives and a community.

Feeling your heart break? Pray for your next step.

To find his next step, Nehemiah prays for his next step. In fact, the only way Nehemiah can get up and overcome his heartbreak in a productive way is through prayer and fasting. Prayer is communication with God. Fasting is a spiritual discipline where one deprives one's self of something while, at the same time, praying for God to reveal God's will and move mightily in one's situation in a much deeper fashion. In this way, fasting is a prayer amplifier. Nehemiah finds himself in an impossible position: his people are suffering, his community is in shambles, he is one thousand miles away in bondage, and his captivity prevents him from going back to do something about it even though that's the only thing on his mind.

Have you ever been caught up in an impossible situation like Nehemiah that is connected to the well-being of countless lives, including your own? One friend's heart broke for a community of poor, undocumented citizens who live ten miles from his church. The impossible situation is that their citizenship status put him and his relief effort at risk and the hostile, larger, affluent community around the church offered him no support. The well-being of those immigrants' lives depended on a small group of people running an underground operation of healing. How did my friend deal with it? Prayer! It was his next step. If you sincerely pray for the next steps, God will make a favorable way for you to help the very people and situations for which your heart breaks.

And so for four months, Nehemiah has intense conversation

with God through deep prayer and fasting. We know that it is four months because in chapter 1, it was the month of Kislev in the twentieth year when the heartbreak took place. In chapter 2, it was in the month of Nisan in the twentieth year when God began opening doors. In the Babylonian calendar, the months of Kislev and Nisan were four months apart, according to our contemporary understanding. Suffice it to say, Nehemiah invests an enormous amount of time and energy in prayer. Through this, he discovers that the favorable way will only come through aligning himself to God's will. He has to surrender his personal wishes for the much broader wishes of God. As Mark Batterson writes in his book *Draw the Circle*: "God is not a genie in a bottle, and your wish is not his command. His command better be your wish" (Grand Rapid: Zondervan, 2012).

There are some things in prayer Nehemiah needs to do to align himself with God's wishes. Some things he needs to do in order to deal with his heartbreak. Likewise, there are things we need to do, individually and congregationally, in order to accomplish the same. We need to:

1. Recognize God as Lord. Nehemiah needs to recognize that God is not just his Savior who can rescue him from the king's palace and return him to Jerusalem to rebuild, but that God is Lord of his life. God is the Ultimate Director, Governor, Ruler, and Guider of his life. Nehemiah has to learn what we need to learn, and that is that when we let God conduct all our affairs, God always makes a way out of no way.

These days, people don't want anyone to be lord of them, let alone lord over them. People want to do what they want to do, when they want to do it, and how they want to do it. They don't want anyone to be the boss of them, let alone the lord. So it seems easier for people to accept Jesus as their Savior and not their Lord. Because if Jesus is Lord, that means that he calls the shots. It means that we have to surrender our will to his.

We pray to God differently depending upon who we think God is. If I am praying to God as my Savior, it might sound something like this: "Lord, you know this alcohol is kicking my butt. That as much as I seek to give it up, it just keeps tracking me down. I need you, Lord, in the name of Jesus, to save me from this condition. I need you, Lord, to rescue me from the desire to even have the taste of alcohol in my mouth. Please liberate me from this condition that ruins me for days."

But if I'm praying to God as my Lord, it might sound something like this: "God, I thank you for being my Life Director, my Ruler, and my Guide. As I begin this new day, I need you to order my steps in accordance with your will. You know, God, that my steps oftentimes get me into trouble. You know that my steps put me in situations and circumstances that cause temptation and despair. But you know, God, that when I yield my will and my ways to what you want for my life that not only do you provide ways of escape, but also you provide ways of direction. Please be Lord of my Life today. Lead me, guide me along the way. For if you lead me, I cannot stray. Lord, let me walk each day with thee. Lead me, O Lord. Lead me."

Do you pray to God as your Savior or your Lord? Or both? For Nehemiah, in his intense period of prayer, God becomes Savior and Lord. And with God as his Lord, Nehemiah can find God plotting the next steps for him!

2. Acknowledge God as God of the covenant. Alignment meant acknowledging God as God of the covenant. The God who keeps God's covenant with those who love God and seek to follow

God's commandments. The God who alone has and can make a way out of no way. In his heartbreak, Nehemiah needs a way out of no way. So he goes to his God in prayer, acknowledging God as the Way Maker.

Parker Palmer, the renowned activist, educator, community organizer, and writer, talks about an old Quaker phrase in his book *Let Your Life Speak* (San Francsico: Jossey-Bass, 2000). The expression is "Way Will Open." This is used when a certain action is felt to be necessary, but no clear path to accomplishing the task is yet known. If we come to God in prayer, the God of the covenant will make a pathway! A way will open! Nehemiah comes to God in prayer. He acknowledges both God and the covenant God has already made with him and the people of Israel. In heartbreak, if positive next steps are going to come to Nehemiah and to us, God must bring them. If a way is going to be made, God has to make the way. From the start, Nehemiah acknowledges God as the God of the covenant, for through the Covenant Maker and the covenant, a ray of hope will shine.

A covenant is a binding agreement between the covenant maker and those who accept the terms of the covenant. It is an agreement that God keeps, even if we break it. There are consequences for breaking it; we miss out on our blessings. But God is always faithful to God's covenant, and when we align with the God of the covenant, God begins to restore. The Old Testament is a collection of stories of covenant making and covenant breaking. God makes covenant, we get excited about it, and then because of sin we decide we are going to go our own way. And we break covenant. The New Testament reminds us that God loves us so much that God made a covenant of grace with us through the life, death, and resurrection of Jesus Christ. Grace that is so loving that God covers our sin even when we don't realize we've messed up. Like Nehemiah, when we acknowledge God as the God of the covenant, we begin to find strength in the midst of heartbreak. For the Way Maker never leaves us or forsakes us! And if we've fallen away from covenant because of life events, outside influences, or our own missteps, God reminds us that if we will just come back to God in obedience, God stands ready to bless us. For it is God's intent, desire, and business to bless God's people and pour out divine love upon us.

Within the covenant, God makes many promises. One is to be with us. Still another is to be for us. Yet another is to provide. When we find our hearts broken, it is the God who already promised us that God would make a way who is the One we need to approach and acknowledge in prayer. As we do this, we begin to establish and reestablish healthy relationship with God—a relationship of trust that will get us through.

Even in heartbreak, God has everything under control. By faith, we must let God have that control. God's covenant reminds Nehemiah of God's power. Covenant reminds me of the blessing of God's Lordship, that God has provided direction all along. It is when we go our own way and get off course that we get into trouble. Covenant reminds us that we can take the next exit and get back on God's highway if we so choose.

3. Intercede on behalf of the vulnerable and defenseless. Nehemiah's request for alignment and for next steps through prayer is made to God day and night on behalf of the people of Israel; the very people Nehemiah's heart breaks for. Oftentimes we are called by God to pray for ourselves, but when our hearts break for others, if we are praying for a favorable way, our attention in prayer must be devoted to those our hearts break for. We must intercede on their behalf until God responds.

I remember being amongst members of a congregation in southeast Washington, DC, one night as they began testifying to the power of prayer. Specifically, they spoke of the time when one of their beloved members became addicted to crack cocaine and for weeks they didn't know where she was or how to find her. They knew she was alive, barely, but they didn't know where she was because her binges took her from place to place. It was extremely difficult to track her down. Not knowing what to do, and worried for her life, they commenced to pray during their regularly scheduled congregational Bible study. Their hearts broke for her. Every Friday night they began to intercede on her behalf by asking God to bring her back safe and healthy. For months they prayed with no response. Then, on one Friday night at the church while they were in the middle of their prayer meeting, the woman they were praying for walked through the doors and asked: "Who is it that keeps praying for me? I have heard in my own prayers somebody praying for me. Your prayers have broken this curse in my life so I could return to God and to you."

Because of your heartbreak, whom are you interceding for and how serious are you in that intercession? Do you pray all day and all night?

4. Confess sin—the sins of others and your own. Praying for next steps, Nehemiah confesses that the broken down walls and burned up gates of Jerusalem are the result of his and his people's insistence on living disconnected from God. He admits that the vulnerable and defenseless condition that his people are in is the result of his and his people's falling out of a healthy relationship with God. We must confess sin and seek God's forgiveness so that we create space for God to use us and to reconcile us all.

When we confess sin and seek God's forgiveness, we ask God

to remove the roadblock that has kept us from him. If we can get rid of the roadblock, we can be present and intimate with our Creator. We live in an age of power cords. There are cords for TVs, phones, laptops, iPads, lights, and so on. From time to time, we use and abuse power cords so much that they can get frayed or disconnected and no longer consistently provide power. A short can result in intermittent or a complete disconnection from power. When we confess sin and seek God's forgiveness, we acknowledge the "short" and ask God to restore full connection to him.

What do you need to confess and ask for forgiveness for so that power might be restored?

5. Trust and depend upon God's promises. Nehemiah prays God's promises back to God on behalf of himself and the people of Israel. Because somewhere in the wellspring of his faith, he believes that God keeps his promises! And so, by faith, Nehemiah recalls God's promises in his prayer to God: "God, you said that if we are unfaithful, you will scatter us to the four winds, but if we return to you and keep your commandments, you will gather us back from wherever we've been scattered and restore us into your presence." No matter how broken we are or how far we turn away from God, if we return to God, God draws us close and makes us whole again.

When we don't trust and depend on God, we take matters into our own hands. That causes us to be even more scattered than we were in the first place. Nehemiah's ancestors were notorious for doing the opposite of what God wanted. God had been so good to the people of Israel, delivering them from Egyptian bondage. But even still, Israel would grow weary of waiting for God's plan for next steps and would take matters into its own hands. And whenever they did, a blessing that was right around the corner often became a very long trip of agony. In Nehemiah's prayer, he recalls to God an instance of his people's lack of trust and dependence on God, which caused an eleven-day trip to the promised land to become a forty-year journey through the desert. The more we rebel against God, the more we will spin our wheels in frustration.

A dear clergy friend of mine who is doing great work in pastoral ministry speaks often to me about wishing that he had obeyed the call of God earlier in his life. For almost twenty-five years, he ran from what God wanted of him. Having finally said yes and now deeply entrenched in work focused on helping people have life and have it more abundantly, he will from time to time lament to me: "Man, if I had only said yes to God earlier, I wonder what all could have happened." When we refuse to align ourselves with God through trusting and obeying God's every word, we cheat ourselves from great possibilities that God is waiting to bestow.

But, thanks be to God, it's never too late. Pray for your next steps!

What do you need to trust and depend on God for right now?

If we do not come to God in prayer immediately after we discover whom our hearts break for, we will not receive the divine road map for whom we need to help and where we need to help them. We will be stuck in the inability to impact change the way God wants change to come.

When congregations actively encourage people to name and claim whom their hearts break for, there needs to be a commitment to prayer for next steps. If the congregation doesn't model the notion that we must seek God's will and guidance for next steps, individuals don't learn how to do the same. You must model what you want to see. You must have seasons where collectively people discern next steps in prayer.

At my church, we have a habit of fasting and praying anytime we are at a fork in the road or a place in our life together where there is lack of unity about what to do next. Years ago, we were divided on whether or not to build a new church building. There were those who felt that our deteriorating 1922 structure should be maintained even when structural engineers told us not to sink any more money into the building. And there were those who didn't just want to build a church building, but wanted to ensure that whatever we did had the congregation and community's best interests and needs at heart. Our hearts broke for people struggling to find a place to live, so our conversations around building a new building always centered around building housing for transient and homeless families as well.

In the midst of our season of prayer and fasting, the church experienced two fires. After the first, a firefighter told us we were twenty minutes from losing everything. The second fire could have blown up our boiler and everything else. It was clear, through divine intervention in the midst of our congregational praying, that God wanted us to build. Build a new place of worship, yes, but build a place that would help those our hearts broke for as well. Those who were all-in stepped forward, and those who were not lagged behind. But it was the season of congregational prayer and fasting that was tantamount to our discerning from God the direction of the next steps.

Congregational prayer and fasting for God's favorable way makes a huge difference. There was a cooperative parish in my district whose collective heart broke for people of many nationalities in their community who were struggling to survive. In

2009, two congregations were put in a cooperative parish, and by 2012, they had experienced much blessing in cooperative ministry. However, they had a lack of unity around what to do about their two burdensome facilities. They were not maximizing the resources God had given them and were wasting valuable dollars on maintaining spaces that could help feed more people in their community. In August of 2013, they intensified their prayer together, asking: "God, who are you calling us to be and do to build your kingdom? What resources (money, people, buildings, and so on) do we need and what do we need to release in order to do that?" During a retreat, it became clear to members that God wanted them to use one facility for disciple making and the other as a mission center for meeting the needs of the community. Most of the people who attended the retreat would later testify that they were amazed at how much they felt that the Holy Spirit had moved as they saw convergence of teammates who had previously held opposing positions.

At that same retreat, a clear vision was given. The divine nature of both the vision and next steps was evident by a unanimous vote (with one abstention) to merge. Both congregations committed to repurpose their land and buildings to better be a movement of Christ's love to the people of the community, feeding all God's people—body, mind, and spirit—so *no one* goes hungry. Prayer was central to their discernment process of God's favorable way. And they understand that discernment must continue as they journey forward into new frontiers of ministry.

What does your congregation need to pray for?

If you sincerely pray for next steps, God will create a favorable way for you to help the very people and situations your heart breaks for.

Personal: Review the steps Nehemiah takes to be on the same page with God in prayer. What do you need to pray for? What needs to change in your prayer life so that your prayers are in line with God's will? Write it down and then begin praying for alignment. Next steps will come.

Small Group: Have people share their discoveries about what they need to do differently in their prayer lives to be aligned with God's will. Keep track of the prayer requests that come out of that discovery. Then as a group begin praying for one another so that God will position you to be able to discover next steps to address your heartbreak. From this point on, you should check in on progress made in people's prayer lives and keep praying for what group members need.

Leadership Team and Congregation: Given what stage your congregation is in, how are you aligning the congregation corporately in prayer with God so that it might discover God's next steps for the congregation's journey?

Tip

Create opportunities for people to experience corporate prayer in worship. For example, create moments of congregational prayer in worship where different leaders lead the congregation in prayer in a way that provides a living example of the five elements in Nehemiah's prayer. Do a church-wide study or time of prayer and fasting to help people go deeper in prayer.

Step 3

Give It Your All

Y ou cannot be fully engaged without giving it your all. You cannot help people rebuild lives or community with a lukewarm or careless effort. At some point God's call for you to deal with your heartbreak and engage yourself in transformative work is going to require that you be passionately "all-in."

They are your servants and your people. They are the ones whom you
have redeemed by your great power and your strong hand.
"LORD, let your ear be attentive to the prayer of your servant and to the
prayer of your servants who delight in honoring your name. Please give
success to your servant today and grant him favor in the presence of this
man!"
At that time, I was a cupbearer to the king.
—Nehemiah 1:10-11

Are You All-In?

Forever Jones articulates this Divine truth powerfully in their song, "He Wants It All." The song starts with a voice crying out in search of a selfless, childlike heart that will love God completely. We then get an image of God walking the earth in search of people who are desperate and in need of love. Love that can only be found in surrendering oneself fully to God and God's will for their lives:

> And he says: Love me, love me with your whole heart
> Serve me, serve me with your life now...he wants it all
> today.

At some point God wants your whole heart and he wants it all. Nehemiah gets to the place where he is prepared to give God his whole heart. At the end of his vocalized prayer in chapter 1, Nehemiah makes it plain that he's all-in: "Please give success to your servant today and grant him favor in the presence of this man!" He is prepared to even put his life on the line to see what God has started in him come to pass.

To get to the point of passionate leadership where you are all-in doesn't happen overnight. In addition to the collection of life experiences, Nehemiah shows us that we have to be willing to allow God to break us down and position us to be the leader God needs us to be. There are three pieces of that process that we see Nehemiah go through:

1. Coming to grips with your past issues. In four months of mourning, fasting, and praying, Nehemiah's got to deal with his past issues until he can come face-to-face with who he has been and who God is. As one who was in the first wave of the exile to Babylon, he has to come to grips with the fact that his sin contributed to his current enslaved condition and the disenfranchisement of his people back home: "**Exile** means to be away from one's home (i.e. city, state or country), while either being explicitly refused permission to return and/or being threatened with imprisonment or death upon return" (en.wikipedia.org /wiki/exile). From a spiritual point of view, exile is the feeling of being disconnected from God, who is our home. When we are in spiritual exile, we feel disconnected from God even though God never disconnects himself from us. Oftentimes our behaviors, habits, or attitudes remove us from feeling the presence of God. The more we act counter to God, the farther away from God we feel. Nehemiah hears the news of what his past transgressions have resulted in and has to go through a spiritual reformation of sorts so that God can have his full attention.

Nehemiah has to embrace the reality that his disenfranchised life from God played a part in Jerusalem's current demise. He has to come to the point where he sees his reality wrapped up in the reality of those back home. And though there are class differences between them, because the poorer class in the exile always got left behind, Nehemiah needs to see himself at one with his poor brothers and sisters back home.

So often today, places across the world—including the United States—are broken, divided, and in disgrace much like Jerusalem was in the book of Nehemiah, because too many leaders have become classist and have not come face-to-face with the full picture of why our current situations are the way they are. And as a result, our leadership is often single-issue driven and oblivious to the welfare of all.

We don't need leaders like this. The world, the church, and communities need passionate leaders like Nehemiah who are willing to do the soul-searching work of identifying who they are in the eyes of God, where they have been with God (the good, the bad, and the ugly), and where God wants to take them and others so that we can all live powerful and productive lives.

2. Becoming at one with God and the people. Nehemiah's present reality is the confusion and alienation of exile. He is in Persia, one thousand miles from Jerusalem. He sees that the entire congregation is scattered. Whenever there was exile in the Old Testament, the raiding country would take the best and brightest as slaves; those who could help strengthen the conquering empire. Those without skills, those who hadn't embraced their gifts, those who were poor, those who had low self-esteem always got left behind. Left behind and trying to preserve the remnant of who they had always been. Yet critical players are now gone. All of this happens in the context of being pressured to conform to the new regime. In today's world, an equivalent of this would be brain drain. Brain drain takes place when the best and brightest of a nation either leave for a brighter opportunity or are recruited out of their country. What's left behind is a nation that struggles and is left vulnerable and defenseless to the whim of leaders who often have their own selfish motives guiding their decision making at the expense of the people.

You can't address heartbreak until you actually go beyond the emotion of the heartbreak and get to the core. You can't begin to embrace the transformation that this work will require unless you see your place in it and are willing to commit yourself passionately to bringing about positive change. You won't get to the place of being all-in with God or with the people you serve until you see yourself at one with God and the people. The reality is there are forces that contributed to the shame and disgrace of Jerusalem; there are forces that played a role in the shame and disgrace you may see in your community right now. And until you own up to participating in that, or at the very least, embracing it fully as your own, those whom your heart breaks for will not see you as an authentic leader. You can't authentically lead *with* people until you go beyond the point of seeing them as objects. You must see them as co-laborers with you to bring about what is just, fair, and true. Nehemiah was in the elite class of Jerusalem. And it was his sin and disobedience as well as those of all classes that contributed to Jerusalem's fall. He had to be willing to embrace this and leave any classist thoughts behind.

If leaders of transformation don't develop their oneness with God and the people they seek to lead, then they will continue to pit people against each other and continue to promote a divided community. And in the words of Jesus Christ: A "house divided against itself shall not stand" (Matthew 12:25 KJV).

3. Surrendering to God's will. Nehemiah has to give up what he wants and embrace what God wants. Nehemiah has to surrender his will to God's will. He has to give up status, elitism, comfort, safety, a measure of wealth, and measure of security about his future. He has to become selfless and other-focused. He has to be willing to do whatever God tells him to do. He has to be all-in.

Nehemiah declared to God that he was all-in. At some point during his personal four-month prayer vigil, he made it known to God that he was prepared to do whatever God wanted him to do for the people of Israel and that he was ready to submit himself to whatever risk God needed him to take in order to receive divine favor and kingly permission and provision. There he was, fully sacrificed to do God's will, to help lead the effort to restore lives and restore Jerusalem. There we must be, fully sacrificed to God to restore the people in our communities for whom our hearts break.

In Nehemiah's situation, being surrendered to God's will requires him to leave the comfort of the king's palace and return to the discomfort of a city reduced to rubble. What does being surrendered to God's will require of you? For me, it required leaving the comfort of a profitable career in communications and returning to one of the communities of my youth—a community ravaged by drugs, alcohol abuse, disenfranchisement, white flight, and economic despair. For you, it will probably mean something else.

But, it's important to understand that Nehemiah's example of passionate leadership didn't happen overnight. Few leaders jump all-in to what God wants in a twinkling of an eye. For Nehemiah, it takes his lifetime to that point plus four months. For me, it took thirty-two years and four months before I surrendered to what God wanted.

When I finally responded to God's call for me to be an ordained minister, it was because God had boxed me in. My heart broke for people who were exiled, who felt disconnected from God because of past sin and because they were more consumed by the ritual of church than they were in a true, authentic, and transparent relationship with Jesus Christ. It pained me deeply to see people who had real-life problems cover them up rather than authentically come to God with their mess and passionately seek God to make it right. And my own friends and I at the time were struggling with real life issues—issues such as family conflict, relational issues, work/life balance issues, and the like—that we knew the word of God had to have answers for.

To really do something about what my heart broke for, I would have to give up my aspiring career in communications. I would also have to deal with the reality of being a man without a job with a wife and two very young children. I would have to give up a boatload of money, plans to increase my wealth and status in the world, and my own personal dreams of a powerful communications career. I would have to allow my will to be shaped into God's will.

Little by little, I found God doing just that. The Bible study I started, which grew from four people to forty, continued to fuel God's call on me to be a pastor. The anxiety of being unemployed, then seriously underemployed for a good period of time, forced me to do what my ancestors used to call, "talk to the Master." I began sincerely engaging in prayer that I hoped would reveal to me a bigger picture of where I was and where God was leading me.

I began to share my pain and pray about this agonizing situation at the Bible study I had formed. For a good year and a half, I began to ask the Lord what he wanted for my life. In that prayer time, God broke me down. I had to listen to the innermost parts of my being. I had to have a conversation with my soul. I had to yield my will to God's will. And I did that through prayer, study, and talking with people, but mostly it was a quiet inner journey marked by prayerful conversation with God and a slow surrender of my will to God's will.

If you don't have a sense of where God is leading you, don't worry! Depending on where you are with God, and depending on whom God assigns to you to serve, it may take time for God to build up an authentic passion within you to lead for a particular purpose. Or, God may give this passion to you all at once. It seems Nehemiah's quest for divine guidance took four months. Ours may take less time or more.

But what is most important here is that we ultimately ask the question: What does it take for us to go all-in? Or what does God have to do to us before we surrender our will to his?

This is a critical question for all of us to answer and for our congregations to answer. The church needs passionate leaders who are surrendered to make learners and followers of Jesus Christ for the transformation of the world. People who are committed to demonstrating the love of Christ through establishing or building a community of love where there is justice and righteousness for all people.

In congregations where leaders are giving it their all, we see unity (not always agreement in all things), focus, long-term commitment, an environment where passionate leadership becomes contagious, and a continuous story being told about where we've been, where we are, and where God is leading us in the future so that exile doesn't happen again.

Many churches are in exile, feeling separated from God. They are in exile not because God has left them, but because the congregation has become more concerned with keeping members happy and comfortable than with what matters to God. As a result, many congregations are dying because they lack the passion to reach new people. They are void of the inspiration to build a community of hope where people can experience God on all levels: spiritually, culturally, economically, and the like.

A couple of summers ago I went with a ministry partner of mine, Christie Latona, to Trinity United Methodist Church in Granite City, Illinois, outside of St. Louis. Trinity's ministry was in a very poor, predominantly white community. Hunger, unemployment, and low-income housing were prevalent. I had never been in a white ghetto before. Trinity found that its heart broke for hungry children and their parents, many of whom lived right under their noses, a few of whom worshipped in their pews. Because their pastor, Lisa Guilliams, had a Nehemiah-like passion, suddenly this small church took its big-time passion outside its doors and began engaging with its community.

Engagement with the community brought a unity to this congregation, which at one point was struggling to survive. It also gave the congregation a singular focus, one that has spread into the creation of a powerful 501c3 called The Family Treehouse, which fed more than fifty thousand people in the summer of 2013, more than double the amount fed the year before. In addition, The Family Treehouse has now led the church to offer worship and small-group opportunities in the very communities where food is being distributed, but where people don't necessarily have a church home. Passionate leadership is central to healing broken hearts and communities.

Are you all-in? This is the question before you. If the answer is yes, the next question for you and your congregation is: What is necessary for your church to give its all for the long haul? In the words of Forever Jones, "He wants it all. God wants it all."

Personal: Are you all-in? If not, which of the three steps in the chapter do you need to take to be all-in?

Small Group: Have people share their discoveries about what they need to do to be all-in. Then have a group discussion and time of prayer for encouraging everyone to do what they need to do to be full participants in God's restoration process. Before launching into that time of prayer, ask for praise reports and continued requests from chapter 2.

Leadership Team and Congregation: What is needed in order for your congregation to be ready to engage itself in the restoration of broken lives and communities?

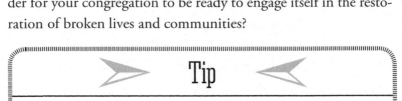

Tip

The leaders of the congregation have to acknowledge the congregation is not all-in with regards to God's restoration process. The congregation has to decide whether it is going to play church or be the church. Usually at this stage church councils or leadership teams have to have a "come to Jesus" meeting with regards to what the congregation is about and what the congregation is going to be known for. Will the congregation be known for mending the hearts of the marginalized in the community or will it be known as a Christian social club that gathers for an hour or two every Sunday morning?

Step 4

Take the Risk

I f you risk positioning yourself for his purposes and use your position for his purposes, God will get you all you need to change lives and communities for the better. You don't have to be in a position of privilege in order to have your position count. Sometimes we don't think our position is significant. Yet when we surrender our agenda to God's agenda, God can use our position to turn things around for the better.

In the month of Nisan, in the twentieth year of King Artaxerxes, the king was about to be served wine. I took the wine and gave it to the king. Since I had never seemed sad in his presence, the king asked me, "Why do you seem sad? Since you aren't sick, you must have a broken heart!"
I was very afraid and replied, "May the king live forever! Why shouldn't I seem sad when the city, the place of my family's graves, is in ruins and its gates destroyed by fire?"
The king asked, "What is it that you need?"

I prayed to the God of heaven and replied, "If it pleases the king, and if your servant has found favor with you, please send me to Judah, to the city of my family's graves so that I may rebuild it."
With the queen sitting beside him, the king asked me, "How long will you be away and when will you return?" So it pleased the king to send me, and I told him how long I would be gone.
I also said to him, "If it pleases the king, may letters be given me addressed to the governors of the province Beyond the River to allow me to travel to Judah. May the king also issue a letter to Asaph the keeper of the king's forest, directing him to supply me with timber for the beams of the temple fortress gates, for the city wall, and for the house in which I will live."
The king gave me what I asked, for the gracious power of my God was with me.
So I went to the governors of the province Beyond the River and gave them the king's letters. The king had sent officers of the army and cavalry with me.
—Nehemiah 2:1-9

Will You Risk Your Position for Good?

Taking risks for God becomes much easier once you have felt your heart break, prayed for next steps, and let God know you are all-in. Once you are all-in, God can use your position, whatever it may be, to position you to get all you need to change lives and communities for the better.

Change doesn't come without taking risks. One of the strongest illustrations of this for me is the story of Vernon Johns. Most people these days have no idea who Vernon Johns is. But suffice it to say, if Vernon Johns had not taken the risk he did, the civil rights movement in America might not have been born.

Vernon Johns was the senior pastor of the Dexter Avenue Baptist Church in Montgomery, Alabama. Dexter Avenue is a prominent African American congregation known in civil rights circles that is housed in a small, redbrick church building. It is located directly across the street from the pantheon-like Alabama Supreme Court and immediately next door to the equally impressive Alabama State Capitol. Picture yourself driving past this church in the early 1950s and seeing the following sermon topic on the highly visible church marquee out front: "It's Safe to Kill Negroes in Montgomery."

That was the title of Vernon Johns's sermon one Sunday in the heat of racial violence in which many blacks lost their lives without any protest or opposition from blacks or consequences handed down to the perpetrators from the white establishment. The title of the sermon, posted and preached, was an extremely risky move for Reverend Johns to take. Not only did he put himself in great danger, right under the nose of Alabama's symbols of white power, but also he was rebuked and scorned by his own congregation, many of whom were afraid that the pastor's actions would bring negative repercussions to them. However, Johns took the risk and used his position as pastor and the position of his church building for good.

And while Johns's risk-taking exploits soon resulted in his departure from the pulpit, it made a way for his successor to begin a quite historic journey leading to justice for multitudes. The successor's name: Dr. Martin Luther King Jr. Without Johns's risk, King would not have become pastor of the first church he ever led. And the civil rights movement as we know it, spurred on by the Montgomery bus boycott, may have never taken place.

When you are seeking to heal broken hearts and communities, the time will come when you must take a risk. Nehemiah

41

took a risk having felt his heart break, having fasted and prayed for next steps, and having decided to give God his all. While risk-taking is never easy, when God inspires it through prayer, you and I can and must take action. Lives are depending on it. Here are some risk-taking tips that Nehemiah offers to us:

1. Make yourself vulnerable. At the end of four months, Nehemiah finds himself serving Chardonnay to the king. While we know Nehemiah has been mourning for four months, this is the first time he allows himself to look sad, the sadness a reflection of his broken heart, but the sadness also serving as an opener for conversation with the king. If we were to imagine the cupbearer functioning much like Forrest Whittaker did in Lee Daniels's movie, *The Butler*, then we'd know that cupbearers did not talk unless requested and they kept their feelings to themselves. Speaking out of turn, or speaking at all, could put them at risk of losing their jobs, or in Nehemiah's case, his life. Nehemiah had to make himself vulnerable before the king because the king was his only avenue to get back to his community, Jerusalem. No one had the human power or the authority to set Nehemiah free to go do what God wanted him to do, except the king. And so Nehemiah did just this. Who do you need to make yourself vulnerable before? And where does your vulnerability need to be seen in order for God to make a way for you to fulfill God's will?

I've had to make myself vulnerable in several fights for justice, spanning from stances against political officials in the city where I serve to positions I've needed to take within the larger church hierarchy. But I couldn't advocate for or even show love toward the people my heart broke for in these respective situations unless I became vulnerable at the moment God needed me to be. This raises a couple of important points:

- You can't love people unless you are willing to be made vulnerable. People see your authenticity and sincerity in your vulnerability, and when they see it in a *Kairos* moment, or "God moment," powerful things can happen. Powerful connections can be made. Closed doors can fling open in a moment!

- You've got to be sure that the moments when you make yourself vulnerable are divinely directed and driven by the Holy Spirit. Why? Because when you open yourself to others in this way, you open yourself to be a transforming agent, but you also open yourself up to be hurt. And while all of us have been hurt and will be hurt, inviting unnecessary pain upon yourself is not something that even God would recommend! You've got to be "prayed up"; you've got to be in a spiritually grounded position where you can see, hear, and feel God leading you to take a risk.

2. Feel the fear and do it anyway. The king, always attentive to the cupbearer's actions and movements, notices Nehemiah's sad countenance and inquires why Nehemiah is in such condition. If you are the king and your cupbearer is having a bad day, you'd ask what's going on, too. Remember, trusting the cupbearer could mean life or death for you. So you inquire!

The king asks Nehemiah why he is so sad. And in the fear of the moment, Nehemiah takes a risk and speaks up. Speaking up could have cost Nehemiah his job, let alone his life. But when you are prayed up and know that God has positioned you for His purposes, you will know when it's time to speak up and when it is time to shut up. It's all right to feel the fear, but when you know it's time to speak up, speak up!

Is it time for you to speak up about something, but you haven't because fear is gripping you? What are you afraid of and

43

what do you need to overcome right now, so that the Lord's desires can proceed?

I recall being in a huge church meeting once where some unethical and unjust decisions were about to be made, and most of the gathered body did not know it. If the decisions went through, it could have put multitudes of people in the possible position of great financial risk. A small group of us did know the consequences, however, and began praying and strategizing over how God might use our position to exact justice in that very critical moment. The voices of some of us in the group had already been silenced, because we'd spoken up already, and the opportunity for us to speak again would be no more. But I'll never forget a colleague of mine standing up at the last moment and offering a speech and a motion that saved the day for many. With courage and a quivering voice, she spoke truth to power. And as Amos the prophet declared, justice rolled down like water and righteousness as an ever-flowing stream (5:24). When it's time to take risks, fear will come. But when you know it's God's time for you to speak up, in the words of the Nike commercials: Just do it!

3. Use your position to get what God wants. When the king asks, "What do you request?" Nehemiah has to pray some more. We imagine him saying, "God, is this the moment that you grant me success? What should I ask for?" It's vitally important that when God opens the door for you, that you pray first for the divine plan. Then use your position for God's purposes. Nehemiah had been praying for a period of four months for this opportunity. Yet when it came, he had to pray some more. It is always good to gain confirmation before taking additional risks.

Biblically, Nehemiah had plenty of company here. God often positioned prophets to use their position to get what God wanted.

God did so with Moses, leading Israel out of bondage. God did it again with Joshua, leading the people to the promised land. God did it still again with Esther, taking a risk to go to the king to thwart an evil plot. God specialized in it with Elijah and Elisha, performing miracle after miracle to provide for God's people in the time of need. With a prayed-up heart, you can use your position to get what God wants so that people who are vulnerable and defenseless in the midst of adversarial activity can be restored!

With God's blessing, Nehemiah asks for everything he needs. Not what he wants, but what he needs to fulfill God's will and respond to the needs of the people in his community. What do you need to fulfill God's will in your community? Do you need the capacity to help people find jobs? Do you need resources to finish a building project? Do you need more volunteers to help children in the schools? Do you need more people to support adults in crisis? Do you need more people with financial expertise to start empowering people economically? Do you need God to simply give you permission to go make it happen? Collectively, we may know the people who can help with these things. Perhaps we are those people.

So Nehemiah asks for permission to be positioned to rebuild the city. Request granted. Nehemiah gave a time frame for his work and when he would return. Request granted. Nehemiah asks for a visa and passport to authorize his travel back home. Request granted. Nehemiah asks for the resources to rebuild the city. Request granted. Nehemiah asks for the resources to build his own house so that he would have a place to stay during his work. Request granted. Nehemiah did not ask for a cavalry escort to protect him along the way, but the king granted it to him anyway. When God opens the door for what you need, prepare yourself to be overwhelmed by God's generosity.

When you position yourself for God's purposes, and use your position for God's purposes, God will grant you favor to change lives and communities for the better.

A congregation's building is in a community for a reason. We are planted in locations for a reason. Positioned to effect transformation for a divine purpose. The things a congregation has to ask God as it is taking a divine risk include:

- What do you want us to do given who you have made us to be?

- What do you want us to do given where you have positioned us in the community?

- Who in our midst have you sent with connections and networks for doing what matters to you?

- Who do we need to connect with in order to acquire the needed human resources and permissions?

When a congregation asks these questions and others that will arise, risks can be taken and requests will be honored. Ultimately, community restoration will come to pass.

My church has been living a risk for the past several years. Its heart has broken for people who cannot find homes to live in, let alone affordable places to stay. After establishing itself as a place for providing transitional housing, as well as providing services for the homeless, the congregation sensed a call by God to do something greater to help families find shelter.

God revealed a vision now called The Beacon Center—a $39 million multipurpose facility that will provide affordable housing, worship, and community space for people in the Brightwood neighborhood of DC and beyond. The vision started as a $3 million project that went to a $9 million project, that's now a $39 million dream of God. We didn't have $3 million; we didn't have $9 million. We certainly don't have $39 million! But God does. And for the past three years, God has been positioning us to take and beckoning us to take risk after risk after risk and has helped us navigate the highly politicized environment of DC politics.

We realized that we were established on the hill where we reside to be a beacon of hope for those hopeless in our community. We realized that we've transitioned from fighting to keeping our doors open to becoming a major community leader in order to be a blessing. Through our connections and networks (some sent to us, others revealed to us—connections that have been Jewish, Christian, agnostic, nonbelievers, and more) God has been using our position to make requests and to receive from the "kings" outside of the church all but $3 million of the $39 million project. The rest is for the church to find. By God's grace, we can do that! It is a miracle; but God is in the miracle-working business, particularly when individuals and congregations pray for God's guidance and take the God-ordained risks as they come!

As we have made ourselves vulnerable and refused to allow fear to stop us, we have discovered God positioning kings and kingly officials to grant our requests. From private meetings that have led to thousands of dollars to press conferences that have yielded multimillions, God continues to open doors for us to join with the residents of our community to build and strengthen Brightwood for everyone's good.

What risk is God asking you to take so that your position can be used for good?

Personal: Yes, it is a redundant, but very personal question:

47

What risk is God asking you to take so that your position can be used for good?

Small Group: Have people share their discoveries about what risks God is asking them to take. Then ask each other the question: How vulnerable before God are you willing to become so that God can use you to change lives in the congregation and community for the better? After this discussion, open prayer time with praise reports and continued needs from previous weeks (prayer and being all-in), adding to it prayers to undergird risk taking. Be sure to pray specifically for people in the group who are making themselves more vulnerable and taking more risks than they ever have before.

Leadership Team and Congregation: What risks are you willing to take and what new ways do you need to lead your congregation to be positioned for community revitalization?

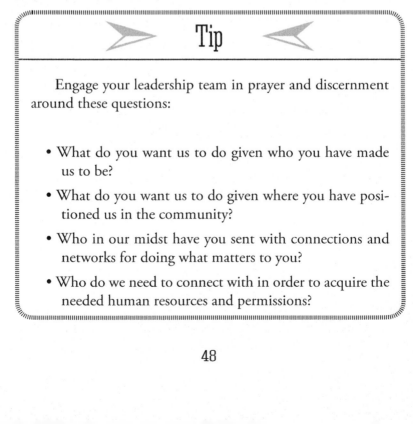

Tip

Engage your leadership team in prayer and discernment around these questions:

- What do you want us to do given who you have made us to be?
- What do you want us to do given where you have positioned us in the community?
- Who in our midst have you sent with connections and networks for doing what matters to you?
- Who do we need to connect with in order to acquire the needed human resources and permissions?

Step 5

Inspect Your Mission Field

Too often we end up doing ministry *for* people instead of *with* people. This happens because of two things: (1) we see an "us" and "them" divide; and (2) we identify a need based on statistics proving what we think needs to be done, instead of building relationships with those in the community and letting them tell us what they will partner with us to accomplish. If, like Nehemiah, we walk before we talk, then when we talk, people will walk with us.

When I reached Jerusalem and had been there for three days, I set out at night, taking only a few people with me. I didn't tell anyone what my God was prompting me to do for Jerusalem, and the only animal I took was the one I rode. I went out by night through the Valley Gate past the Dragon's Spring to the Dung Gate so that I could inspect the walls of Jerusalem that had been broken down, as well as its gates, which had been destroyed by fire.

Then I went on to the Spring Gate and to the King's Pool. Since there
was no room for the animal on which I was riding to pass, I went up
by way of the valley by night and inspected the wall. Then I turned
back and returned by entering through the Valley Gate.
The officials didn't know where I had gone or what I was doing. I
hadn't yet told the Jews, the priests, the officials, the officers, or the rest
who were to do the work.
—Nehemiah 2:11-16

What Does Your Inspection Reveal?

The one whose name means "The Lord Has Comforted" has now returned to the people and the place he must comfort in this season of his life. And Nehemiah must comfort a people who, like Nehemiah in exile, have become comfortable with their conditions and their surroundings even though they are defined by disgrace.

The church in the Western hemisphere in many respects has grown comfortable. We've grown comfortable because we've lost sight of our ecclesiastical origins and we've lost focus on what the mission of Jesus Christ was in the first place. We've spent more time gazing at and maintaining our cathedrals of worship than we have investing in and caring for the well-being of people as a whole. Or if the church means people to us, it means people we already know and are comfortable with.

From the beginning of what we know as church, Pentecost, the mission of Jesus Christ was about relationship building, sharing the good news of Jesus with others, and committing ourselves to meeting the needs of those in community. That was the model and the power of the Acts 2 church. Change was happening daily. New life was being discovered daily. Transformation of lives was taking place daily. Day by day, we are told, people were being added to the fellowship, to the church. Community needs were being met: any one who lacked, someone else filled the void. And signs and wonders of God's presence were seen everywhere. In the early church there was no distinction between church and the mission field—they were one and the same.

When Nehemiah returns to Jerusalem—the City of Peace—it doesn't appear that any community building is taking place. He's been told by his brother and his boys in the hood that all is not well. It is one thing to hear bad news from others; it is another to see and inspect it for yourself. And since Nehemiah had come home not to a big homecoming reception, but on a mission from God to heal broken hearts, walls, gates, and communities, an inspection of his mission field was surely in order.

If the church is going to effectively engage with the community around it, which by biblical origin we have been commanded and shown how to reach, we must spend time seeing, hearing, feeling, touching, embracing, and loving our mission field. We must behave as if the community is our congregation. The streets are our sanctuary. The back alleys are our altars of blessing. Farmlands are our fields of opportunity. New housing developments become our narthex through which new life is ushered. And strip malls of suburbia become creative places for leading people to salvation. As John Wesley put it, the world is our parish.

With God's provision and the king's permission, Nehemiah heads to Jerusalem to rebuild the city's broken-down walls and its gates destroyed by fire. As soon as Nehemiah arrives, he chills for three days. When he hits the ground, he doesn't go to the temple or the synagogue—he starts walking the streets. He doesn't have the luxury of pulling out his laptop and downloading the latest MissionInsite report. Instead, he decides to get out of the house and walk the streets at night. You discover what is really going on in a city when you walk the streets at night. You find out who's hanging out and who's not. Where the hot spots are and where they aren't. Where trouble is brewing and where there's peace. Where stuff is broken and where it's really broken. Who runs the streets from their home and who runs it from the corner. You learn a lot about your mission field when you take time to inspect it by night. And for those of you who live in small towns or the countryside where things are quiet at night, a nighttime inspection provides anonymity and privacy from people who are constantly on the lookout and suspicious about anyone looking around.

Nehemiah sets out at night, under cover, in the dark, so that no one can see him. He keeps his divine revelations close to him so that no one can compromise what God is up to. When you open your mouth too fast, you can compromise divine vision.

But Nehemiah doesn't go out to inspect alone. He takes a few others with him so that they can see what he sees. He takes trusted people who he can bounce ideas off of, and who can bounce ideas off of him. You can't take just anybody with you on your inspection. You've got to take people who are with you through thick and thin—not people who just tell you they are with you and then disappear, but people who are truly with you and show it by their deeds. We've got enough talkers in the world; we need some walkers.

Nehemiah doesn't let anyone else know where he's going or

what he's doing. Because he knows, like we do, that the text-message nation, Facebook families, and Twitter tribes would go crazy if they found out too soon.

By night, Nehemiah examines the walls of Jerusalem and each of the gates. Intimately, personally, and carefully, he inspects his mission field. He surveys by horse, and then when the horse can't go any further because of the rubble, he surveys by foot. Not only do you need to do a drive-by inspection but also you need to get out of your car, walk in the necessary places and spaces, walk with and in people's lives, and see what's going on in your broken-heart situation. Nehemiah sees it for himself, because you have to walk before you talk.

While it seems to have taken Nehemiah only one night to conduct his inspection, it will no doubt take you much longer. But no matter how long it takes, perform the due diligence necessary to get all the information you need before moving forward. Only after Nehemiah gathers his personal information, compiles the sad truths, but sees the hidden possibilities in Jerusalem, does he go public.

You've got to get to know your community and let your community get to know you. This does not have to be a complex process—it can be done simply. For example, I conduct prayer services in the gym where I exercise when called upon. I preach and conduct prayer meetings at the family support collaborative down the hill from Emory. Like us, there are other folks in the trenches who need the holistic support of the church to make it through life's challenges.

You must constantly inspect your community. Get to know it like the back of your hand. If I stop in your community and ask someone if he or she knows your church and what your church is known for, he or she should be able to tell me—and what he or she tells me ought to be positive. Your congregation and community need to have a great marriage together. But for that to happen, there's got to be a first date, then many dates afterward, and then an engagement and a *marriage*, not just a wedding.

Here are four steps congregations must take in order to conduct a thorough community inspection.

1. Conduct relational interviews. You and your people must engage yourselves in doing one-on-one relational meetings. I learned this through watching my family interact with their communities in DC, Pittsburgh, Philadelphia, New Orleans, and the Los Angeles and Oakland areas. I also learned the importance of this through immersing myself in various training opportunities related to community development and community organizing, like the Communities of Shalom, which is a United Methodist initiative, and the Industrial Areas Foundation (IAF), which organizes people and money with churches and communities to leverage for power to address social justice issues. One-on-one relational meetings are foundational to conducting a useful inspection.

To identify with whom and where you need to begin the one-on-ones, you need to identify a particular area or boundary in which you are going to interview people. For example, you may decide to talk with everybody within a very small radius of your church. Or you might make that radius wider and select people in particular sectors to begin your interviews with, like those in schools, businesses, and associations. As you talk with these people, ask them basic questions to get to know them, as you allow them to get to know you. You'll discover that you have far more in common with the people in your neighborhood than you ever imagined. You'll also discover names of others in your community whom you need to interview. For example, one person I started with was the director of the private school that leased out space in our church. This led me to other educators and leaders in the neighborhood and served as the springboard for my relational meetings in the neighborhood.

These interviews provide a time where you can get to know people and allow people to get to know you. In addition, you can take note of people's passions, dreams, and desires—not just for their lives, but also for the communities in which they live. As you get to know people, these one-on-one relational meetings become an opportunity to reach people for Jesus and to develop new members in the congregation as the Holy Spirit guides. But the key factor here is simply building relationships so that community can be formed.

Ask basic questions such as:

• Where are you from?

• How did you get here?

• How long do you see yourself here?

• What would you like this community to become?

• What is your perception of our church?

• How can we help you or help the community achieve your vision?

These questions will open the door to conversations that will blow your mind. They'll also position you and the person you are talking with to feel what the other feels, experience what the other experiences, and at some point, begin taking steps to make transformative community partnerships. Do *not* use these interviews to "sell" the church to the person you are talking with, nor use them as an evangelization tool. Let God take care of the relationship and the direction in which it travels. After each conversation, you need to make notes to help you keep track of what you've learned.

In Nehemiah's community transformation process, it was through this type of relationship building that he was later able to inspire the people to do what they collectively needed to do.

2. Understand community demographics. You need to gather and get to know your community demographics intimately. While the one-on-one relational meetings provide you with firsthand accounts, you need to research your community's demographics so that you have a broader understanding of the community trends that are taking place in your neighborhood. For example, you need to confirm who is in your community through these studies. You may see it firsthand yourself, but I guarantee you there are a host of people you don't even know about in your community. You need to find out who they are. All of these demographic studies rely on census data, so many elements of the population may not be accurately represented.

One tool that is useful in understanding how your community demographics might impact your church is the Mission Impact Guide (v. 2.0) by Tom Bandy available through MissionInsite and based on Experian data. Bandy has written this with a church lens so that you can discover the religious perspectives of the people in your community and what kind of small groups, leadership, hospitality, and outreach they prefer.

3. Identify your "mayors." While you are studying your demographics and conducting your one-on-one relational meetings, you will discover who the "mayors" are in your community. I'm not just talking about your actual mayor or other elected officials. Obviously, you should know who the elected officials are in your community—you will need them and they will need you down the road—but as you are talking with people in your community, you will discover who the real mayors are. These are the people of influence that even the elected officials unofficially report to. These are the people who know your community better than anybody.

They know who you are, and you haven't even met them yet. These are the people who sit on their front porches, play checkers on the front stoop, hang out in the barber shops, beauty salons, feed supply stores, ball courts, and local hangouts who can tell you everything happening in your neighborhood, when it is happening, how it is happening, who is doing it, who it benefits, and who it hurts. These folks can trigger the start of any project, or they can kill any project. They can put a good word out about your church, or they can influence people to not even be bothered with your church. Church leaders *must* get to know these mayors intimately and seek to win them over to our team—even if they never worship in our churches. Why? Because they can greatly impact the growth and development of our congregations and communities.

These individuals are powerful people, and they may go to church or they may not. They may be Christian, Jewish, Muslim, or may not declare any kind of faith. They may be homeless or professional, blue collar or white collar, male or female, gay or straight, they may be gangbangers, drug lords, or simply grandmas or grandpas who've been in the neighborhood longer than anybody. They may be from any number of nationalities or ethnic groups. But you've got to get to know them.

In our community, there have been three mayors among many mayors that I've been particularly drawn to. One is a homeless man named Bill. Bill's mom lives in the neighborhood, but Bill, for various reasons, seeks to spend periods of time living on the street. Bill knows everybody and everything. In fact, when my hubcaps were stolen off my car twice in one month, I asked Bill if he knew who did it. Within a few days Bill knew who did it and where they were. He said, "Pastor, I found out who stole your hubcaps, but you won't have to worry about them because the police found them, and they're gonna be locked up for a good little while." Later on, Bill and I developed such a close bond that he appeared to know my every movement. One day I came into the office, and five minutes later Bill showed up and said, "Pastor, I just want you to know that I know when you come in and when you go out. And I want you to know, we got your back." It is important that you build relationships with people like Bill.

Another mayor in my area is a woman named Kathy Brown. For years, she has provided critical leadership for the major community association in our neighborhood. Kathy's influence reaches from city hall to the surrounding street corners. She passionately cares about her community. Nothing is done unless Kathy is consulted. And her word can convince mayors, council members, developers, and leaders of boards and commissions to do the right thing in our community. You need to get to know the Kathys in your neighborhood.

Still another is an older woman, Ms. Wilson. Ms. Wilson has been volunteering for years for our community's long-standing Meals On Wheels program, which serves hot meals to homebound seniors in our community. Everybody knows Ms. Wilson because she sponsors a host of educational programs for the community—particularly for seniors. Because seniors represent a strong voter block and have more free time on their hands than most people, they are a powerful force in the community's ability to revive itself. You need to get to know the Ms. Wilsons in your world as you work with them to develop and redevelop community.

4. Conduct house meetings. Your relational interviews, demographic research, and relationships with the mayors in the community will position you for the next critical step in community inspection: the implementation of house meetings. A house meeting is a gathering of people with whom you have already conducted relational interviews. Gather people around a common theme or issue that resonates with them. The one-on-one meetings you've had will reveal the common theme or thread. The house meeting itself will provide the opportunity for people to begin strategizing about how the issue or need can be addressed. And when you conduct these meetings, or when others in your congregation do, you want to be sure to bring some of your potential congregational leaders into this process. Oftentimes these house meetings are key to an emerging vision.

In order to make house meetings a success, there are three things that should be planned for: food, note taking, and gathering contact information. Don't be afraid to prepare some food. Some of Jesus's best ministry was done around a common meal or other eating opportunities. Second, be sure to bring an easel, flip-chart paper, and markers so that you can take notes and record the main points shared in the meeting. And third, make sure everyone signs in and includes at least their first and last name and phone number or e-mail address so that people can keep in touch with one another, get the minutes from the meeting, and be alerted to future meeting dates.

These meetings should be no longer than two hours and should be held in a place and space where people feel comfortable. No more than fifteen to twenty people is a good size so that you can easily meet in somebody's home or a favorite neighborhood hangout. The purpose of the meeting is to talk—based on information collected—about shared dreams, visions, and images of what you want the community to become. The meetings are powerful because they enable multiple constituencies to discover common ground.

House meetings like these position you to attract more potential community leaders and even more congregants. Because many participants in the house meetings may not be connected to a congregation, they'll find yours appealing and inviting because you have taken time to invest in them and their community. Frankly, many congregations and pastors are not holding house meetings because they are a lot of work or because they have never learned how to do this. But if you take the time to meet and to teach your people to do it, people in your community who have frowned on the church will begin to embrace the church because you are meeting needs. And that's what Jesus did—he met needs!

What does your inspection reveal?

Personal: There are two different paths you might take. You may either be called to lead a community inspection or participate in one. Which path are you on? And what did your inspection reveal?

Small Group: Have people share their discoveries about the inspection. Make notes of common themes and then pray together.

Open prayer time with praise reports and continued needs from previous weeks (prayer, being all-in, risk taking). Add prayers for the mission field.

Leadership Team and Congregation: Determine what needs to be done to fulfill the steps required for the inspection. Then put in place a plan of action to see that the inspection of your targeted mission field is completed.

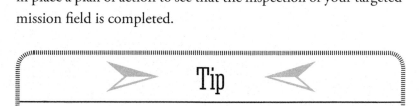

Tip

An inspection often starts with a study of demographics. Task a team with getting a handle on the demographics in your community. MissionInsite provides not only the census data and trends but also Mosaic profiles that give insight to churches on how to best engage particular segments of the population within a particular walk or drive time. The team also needs to do window/windshield demographics, driving around and seeing what your community looks like, as well as a walking tour where it actually interacts with folks and observes native habits and routines.

Step 6

Gain Commitment

When we serve those for whom our hearts break, when we pray for God's next steps, when we're all-in, take risks, and take the time to inspect our mission field, we soon discover that gaining the commitment of others is possible and necessary, particularly when we are prayerful and strategic about it. Before Nehemiah surveyed the situation, he saw himself as one of the community. This enabled him to speak the truth and summon the people to rise up.

So I said to them, "You see the trouble that we're in: Jerusalem is in ruins, and its gates are destroyed by fire! Come, let's rebuild the wall of Jerusalem so that we won't continue to be in disgrace." I told them that my God had taken care of me, and also told them what the king had said to me.
"Let's start rebuilding!" they said, and they eagerly began the work.
—Nehemiah 2:17-18

What Needs to Be Shared to Gain the Commitment of Others?

If you were to travel through communities throughout the United States, let alone across the world, you could see what needs to be done. You can go into some communities and see weedy farmland, dilapidated homes, rusted-out equipment, run-down school buildings, people hanging out on street corners and in bars, and you know that something isn't quite right.

I remember as a teenager traveling to Pittsburgh to see my grandparents during the time when the steel mills were beginning to close. There was a day when I could smell the steel seventy miles outside of town. It was a distinct smell that would get in our clothes and our skin when we would sweat on the Hill District neighborhood playgrounds. But when I returned on one occasion, after having just finished graduate school, there was little to no smell of steel. Many men were unemployed, hanging out on street corners. Jimmy's Bar and Lefty's Tavern—two prominent watering holes in the neighborhood—overflowed with people seeking to drink away their economic misery.

But sometimes the broken walls and burned-down gates in our communities aren't easily seen. Yet in every community, there are people who are vulnerable, defenseless, and at the mercy of an enemy. In some of the most affluent places, those vulnerabilities might be addictions, domestic violence, abuse, children who don't feel loved, children who feel like they don't belong, and the list goes on and on. These hidden problems may take much more time to come out in a community inspection because people aren't readily talking about them. People with real, visible issues don't seem to have as much of a problem talking about them. Nine times out of ten, you don't have to ask a person who is homeless if they are homeless, but if you ask a person who suffers from domestic violence what they think the pressing issues are in their community, he or she more than likely is not going to tell you about his or her misery.

Seeing trouble doesn't necessarily mean that you or I are going to get people to rise up and do something about it. After all, underneath that trouble are stories, systems, and perhaps scandals that keep things the way they are. Shonda Rhimes and Olivia Pope of the television show *Scandal* could have a field day here! And many people have gotten comfortable surviving or existing with the status quo. Gaining the commitment of people to change their lives and situations for the better requires some detailed and specific efforts by at least one or more passionate people to get folks to see what is, what can be, and what's necessary to get there. Passionate people must make others see that they must be participants in making change happen. It takes at least one passionate person whose heart has broken over the trouble, and who is compelled by God to do something about it, to enlist others to help bring about transformation.

That's where we find Nehemiah in 2:17. He has surveyed the situation. He has inspected his mission field. And he has a pretty good idea of what's happening and what needs to be done to rebuild Jerusalem. He has seen firsthand the broken walls and burned-down gates all around the city. He has observed and heard the chatter of political officials and private businesspersons who are capitalizing on the demise of others. Even in the most struggling of neighborhoods, somebody is profiting and doing alright for him- or herself.

Nehemiah has personally felt the pain of disenfranchisement, and after just three short days of dreaming and one long night of inspection, he's ready to enlist others to join him in doing something about it. He's ready to gain their commitment.

Perhaps this is where you are in your church and community. Perhaps this is where you are in your personal prayer life and walk with Jesus Christ. Perhaps you haven't gotten others involved yet because you haven't known how. Well, guess what? Because of God working through Nehemiah, that's all about to change!

To gain people's commitment a series of steps is required.

1. Know their self-interest. One of the basic tenets of community organizing is identifying people's self-interests. Nehemiah did that homework starting back in chapter 1 when he spoke to his brothers about the folks back home in Jerusalem and completes it during his inspection of the current mission field. This is such a critical step that it cannot be skipped. Many people bypass this step, minimizing its importance. But you are not going to be able to speak to people's souls let alone gain their commitment to do something until you know their heart, what causes their heart to break, and what piece of it they are called to touch.

Lonise Bias is a very prominent figure in the Washington metropolitan area who speaks to young people and adults about the ill effects of drugs on families and society. She has done this work for more than twenty-five years. More than twenty-five years ago, you probably wouldn't have found her doing such. But when approached by anti-drug abuse advocacy groups after losing two sons to drug-related issues, one being the former Boston Celtics' first-round draft choice, Len Bias, her heartbreak and sense of mission were aligned with theirs. It didn't take much to gain the commitment of Lonise Bias to do all that she could to make sure other families would not experience the same pain due to drug abuse that her family had experienced.

2. Wait to speak until the time is right. It is worth noting that in his inspection of his mission field, we do not hear Nehemiah opening his mouth to say anything until now. He doesn't speak until *kairos* comes—a moment where God breaks into real time and has everything aligned.

As with other steps, it is critical that you do not skip this step. Timing is everything. If you speak too soon you can lose the opportunity to gain people's commitment. If you wait too long to open your mouth, you can lose the opportunity to gain people's commitment. Timing is everything. And you must be engaged in prayer with God, depending on his grace to know when *kairos* time has come.

As a kid you may have played with dominoes, not matching dots, but standing them in a line and knocking them over to create a chain reaction. The key to creating the maximum impact for your efforts is lining up as many dominoes as possible before knocking the first one over. Timing, layout, and patience are key. Those who seek to rush the layout end up losing. The tiles fall too soon and too few fall. But those who are patient and wait until the dominoes are in the right position and are able to discern the time for the maximum effect end up winning. Timing and patience are everything. So it is with casting a vision or communicating the change that must be done. Discernment is everything; and speaking at the right time can make the difference between lives restored and lives languishing in suffering.

3. Get folks in the community to see you as one of them. Notice the language in 2:17. Nehemiah says: you see the trouble *we* are in. Though he's been one thousand miles away in exile, he communicates like he's one of the Jerusalemites; like he's been there all along and shares ownership of the trouble and disgrace in the community. We can only imagine the passion with which Nehemiah spoke the reality of the situation to the people. It had to have been like he was one of them and that Jerusalem meant as much to him as it did anybody else. When people see your passions and interests are aligned with their self-interests, they will be more inclined to listen to what you have to say and to search their souls as to whether they need to come along with you in this new endeavor.

Former president Bill Clinton had an amazing gift when he was running for office that made you feel like he knew your situation and was one of your own family members. He was quick to tell stories about the people he met along the campaign trail, as if he had spent years with them, not just a few moments. In doing so, he created a sense of "we." And in spite of moral transgressions, this unique ability continues to endear him to the American public.

Being one with the people is who Jesus was, and continues to be. Jesus's knack for being able to communicate with people across the social spectrum, with the religious elite and yet with prostitutes and crooks, gave him the infectious ability to cause people to believe that Jesus knew everything about them. Which he did! But the language that he used was always matched to what people could understand, and his stories were always told in the context of the reality that people lived in. So, when he invited people to a new and better life, it was easy for people to make a decision. The disciples were so impacted that the scripture tells us that they dropped everything and followed him. When you make people feel like you are a part of them, they will go the extra mile with and for you.

4. Share the simple truth of the matter. Nehemiah gets right to the point with a simple one-sentence report to the people: We are in a bad way—Jerusalem is a mess, everything is ruined and burned up. Houston, we have a problem. There comes a time when the passionate leader must cut to the chase and tell folks what the deal is. And you don't need a lot of details to do that. If you had to sum up your community's reality in one sentence, what would that be? What do trouble and disgrace look like in your congregation's neighborhood? It may not be readily seen in your neighborhood the way Nehemiah easily sees the mess in Jerusalem, but if you inspect your mission field thoroughly, you are going to find some kind of mess. You've got to candidly speak it, but only after you've done your homework, after God has brought you to a *kairos* moment and after the people feel you are one of them. If you share the simple truth of the matter and have skipped even one of these steps, it may not be received well or at all.

Too often in congregations, when casting a broad vision of the direction their body needs to take, leaders deliver a message that is too complex, with too many components. There's everything in it, plus the kitchen sink, and people aren't quite sure where to start. Or people are not hearing one unified message; they are only hearing what they want to hear so that they can do what they want to do. While Bill Clinton had the knack of making you feel like "we," similarly Ronald Reagan was profound in his ability to communicate one message. While I was not a fan of Reagan, and being a Washingtonian, still refer to our local airport as National Airport, not Reagan National, which is its official name, no one can really argue against the fact that Reagan was a master at staying on message. In fact, he defeated Jimmy Carter really with one message: "Are you better off today than you were four years ago?"

Republicans still seek to use the simple message strategy in their campaigning today. Whether it was in a speech or on a radio broadcast or in any other communication, Reagan was always brief and to the point. You knew the problem; you knew the opportunity. He was always very clear, whether you agreed with him or not.

What Nehemiah does for the people of Jerusalem is to create a single, simple path to their transformation. When you are able to do this, people are able to get onboard quickly.

5. Extend an invitation. Once Nehemiah shares the simple truth, he extends a simple two-part invitation in an effort to solidify the people's commitment. The first is to join him in rebuilding the walls of Jerusalem. The second is to pursue a passionate life of grace. The first will require manual labor—the sweat equity of the people—to make it happen. The second will demand spiritual labor—the tilling of the soul that will move people to surrender their hearts once again to the God who had saved their ancestors time and again. The gracious God who was now prepared to do it again. "Come—let's build the wall of Jerusalem and not live with this disgrace any longer" (Nehemiah 2:17 *THE MESSAGE*). Powerful, life-transforming action takes place when there is a healthy marriage between manual labor and spiritual labor. When we perform manual labor that is informed by the spirit within, then the labor is not just work that makes us feel good or that is necessary, but work that also accomplishes God-given purposes.

Far too frequently, congregations are doing manual labor—like fixing sandwiches to take to feed homeless people, packing barrels filled with medical and health kits to ship to needy communities overseas, manning clothing closets to give away garments during the winter, or the like—without any spiritual connection to what they are doing. What's needed for transformation is an invitation to offer a spiritual and tangible witness that can change lives and renew hope in the hearts of many.

When Jesus invited people to be whole, he often did so by meeting a tangible need that was followed by or enveloped in a spiritual truth. And when people accepted the invitation, their lives were never the same.

What does your two-part invitation sound like? What is so important here is that people need to make invitation a habit. So often we will invite our friends to parties and social gatherings, but we struggle to invite people to do ministry, to worship, to encounter God, to make their conditions better, and to make the community better. Our Christian faith is grounded in invitation. Jesus invited Peter to become a fisher of men. When we extend an invitation to someone, seeking to gain his or her commitment, we could be inviting someone to lead or participate in the resurrection of multitudes.

6. Share your story of God at work in this situation. After sharing a really short truth and extending a very brief invitation, Nehemiah spends the bulk of his time talking to the people about the wonderful works of God. Specifically, he tells them of how he experienced the hand of God:

- God got my attention.

- God revealed to me that my heart breaks for the people of Jerusalem and the community of Jerusalem, who were vulnerable and defenseless because of the conditions of their community.

- God brought me back in line with his word.

• God restored me into covenant.

• God gave me grace before the king.

• God moved the king to give us everything we need to rebuild.

• Now it's up to us.

In everything God does to move you to engage with your community, God will give you a story to tell. You must tell it. For in the sharing of your story, you will inspire even more people to commit themselves to work with you in the rebuilding. They will roll up their sleeves and get busy because they have felt your heart in their heart and, like you, want to pursue the heart of God. When God wants you to do something, there will always be grace-filled evidence that that is the case.

What stories of God's amazing grace need to be shared within the circles of your congregation and community that are tied into the invitation you just offered? Which testimonies are fueling you to do something about that which breaks your heart? What stories, if they are told, will rally people to pursue something greater than themselves? Share your story when it's time.

One of the most moving stories of a church leader gaining the commitment of a congregation and community to rebuild its walls is that of Bishop Vaughn McLaughlin in Jacksonville, Florida, who two decades ago started a congregation in his house that has now become the Potter's House in Jacksonville and organized a nationwide network of churches called Covenant Fellowship. One week I went to visit Bishop McLaughlin to learn about his fellowship and see the amazing things he was doing in his community. In a half-day, I witnessed a passionate leader in love with the church, in love with its people, devoted to reaching those who did not yet know the Christ, and incredibly concerned about the well-being of the city of Jacksonville.

He took me to the Bible study that he leads for other pastors in Jacksonville. He poured into those leaders for two hours—including principles of community and congregational transformation. He then spent two hours pouring into me, helping me dream dreams and see new visions. That evening, we then went to church and worshipped with his congregation. I learned that the church had acquired a rundown shopping center and was maintaining some of the stores in it but was building an entirely new mall, partnering with new businesses to come into their neighborhood, and establishing a new worship facility in an old supermarket space.

What blew my mind more than anything about this half-day visit was observing what happened after the evening worship service. It was ten days before their move-in date and still much work had to be done to complete the sanctuary. Instead of depending on outside contractors, the gathered congregation that evening—several hundred people—left worship in their old facility and went to what would be their new facility. At 10:00 p.m., they began working to rebuild those walls. It was a fascinating sight. Doctors were painting walls next to ex-convicts. Schoolteachers were laying carpet with their students. White and black folks were installing chairs. Electricians were installing light fixtures with the help of those who would one day apprentice. The bishop himself rolled up his sleeves and handed me a paint roller to work with him. We worked until 11:30 that night. And as God would have it, a member of my congregation who was visiting a relative in Jacksonville for Thanksgiving would attend opening worship in this new facility ten days later. When we are able to gain the commitment of others, people will not only have a mind to work, but people will also work miracles.

What needs to be shared to gain the commitment of others?

Personal: What can you share to gain the commitment of others?

Small Group: Have people identify potential leaders within the congregation and community and develop a plan of action (who, what, when, where, how, why) to gain their commitment based on the steps in the chapter and what people in the group have identified as skills they can share. Open prayer time with praise reports and continued needs from previous weeks (prayer, being all-in, risk taking, mission field), adding to it prayers for gaining commitment.

Leadership Team and Congregation: Determine what needs to be done to fulfill the steps required for gaining commitment. Then put in place a plan of action to seek the commitment of others.

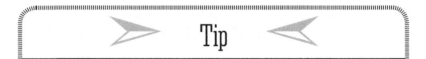

Tip

Articulate the trouble the community is in that needs the congregation's help and do it in a way that taps into the heartbreak of the congregation. You may need to conduct more Relational 1:1 Campaigns and do more community inspection until you have a really good idea of what the congregation and community's self-interest is. Get your leadership team to distill the data into a few key interests for each group. Articulate strategies for addressing these areas. And don't forget to extend an invitation to join in the work and to share your story of God at work in this situation.

Step 7

Get to Work

A ny community engagement effort requires strong organization. People need to know what their assignments are and what is expected of them. Additionally, folks need to learn how to stay In their lane while supporting the common good.

Then Eliashib the high priest set to work with his fellow priests and built the Sheep Gate. They dedicated it and set up its doors, then dedicated it as far as the Tower of the Hundred and as far as the Tower of Hananel. The people of Jericho built next to them, and Zaccur, Imri's son, built next to them. The children of Hassenaah built the Fish Gate; they laid its beams and set up its doors, bolts, and bars. Next to them Meremoth, Uriah's son and Hakkoz's grandson, made repairs. Meshullam, Berechiah's son and Meshezabel's grandson, made repairs next to them, and Zadok, Baana's son, made repairs next to them. Next to them the people from Tekoa made repairs, but their officials wouldn't help with the work of their supervisors.

Joiada, Paseah's son, and Meshullam, Besodeiah's son, repaired the Mishneh Gate; they laid its beams and set up its doors, bolts, and bars. Next to them repairs were made by Melatiah the Gibeonite, Jadon the Meronothite, and the people of Gibeon and of Mizpah, who were ruled by the governor of the province Beyond the River.

Uzziel, Harhaiah's son, one of the goldsmiths, made repairs next to them; and Hananiah, one of the perfumers, made repairs next to him. They restored Jerusalem as far as the Broad Wall. Next to them Rephaiah, Hur's son, ruler of half the district of Jerusalem, made repairs. Next to them Jedaiah, Harumaph's son, made repairs opposite his house, and Hattush, Hashabneiah's son, made repairs next to him. Malchijah, Harim's son, and Hasshub, Pahath-moab's son, repaired another section and the Tower of the Ovens. Next to them Shallum, Hallohesh's son, ruler of half the district of Jerusalem, made repairs, along with his daughters.

Hanun and the people of Zanoah repaired the Valley Gate; they built it and set up its doors, bolts, and bars. They also repaired fifteen hundred feet of the wall, as far as the Dung Gate.

Malchiah, Rechab's son, ruler of the district of Beth-haccherem, repaired the Dung Gate. He rebuilt it and set up its doors, bolts, and bars.

And Shallum, Col-hozeh's son, ruler of the Mizpah district, repaired the Spring Gate. He rebuilt and covered it, and set up its doors, bolts, and bars. He also built the wall of the Pool of Shelah of the King's Garden, as far as the stairs that go down from David's City.

After him, Nehemiah, Azbuk's son, ruler of half the Beth-zur district, repaired from the point opposite David's tombs as far as the artificial pool and the Warriors' House. After him, the Levites made repairs: Rehum, Bani's son, and next to him Hashabiah, ruler of half the district of Keilah, made repairs for his district. After him, their relatives made repairs: Binnui, Henadad's son, ruler of half the district of Keilah. Next to him, Ezer, Jeshua's son, ruler of Mizpah, repaired another section opposite the ascent to the armory at the Angle. After him, Baruch, Zabbai's son, thoroughly repaired another section from the Angle to the door of the house of the high priest Eliashib. After him, Meremoth, Uriah's son and Hakkoz's grandson, repaired another section from the door to the back of Eliashib's house.

After him, the priests from the surrounding area made repairs. After them, Benjamin and Hasshub made repairs opposite their house. After them, Azariah, Maaseiah's son and Ananiah's grandson, repaired beside his house. After him, Binnui, Henadad's son, repaired another section from the house of Azariah to the Angle and to the corner. Palal, Uzai's son, repaired from the point opposite the Angle and the tower projecting from the upper house of the king at the court of the guard. After him, Pedaiah, Parosh's son, and the temple servants living on Ophel made repairs up to the point opposite the Water Gate to the east and the projecting tower. After them, the people of Tekoa repaired another section opposite the great projecting tower as far as the wall of Ophel. From the Horse Gate, the priests made repairs, each one opposite his own house. After them, Zadok, Immer's son, made repairs opposite his own house. After him, Shemaiah, Shecaniah's son, the keeper of the East Gate, made repairs. After him, Hananiah, Shelemiah's son, and Hanun, Zalaph's sixth son, repaired another section. After them, Meshullam, Berechiah's son, made repairs opposite his own room.
After him, Malchiah, one of the goldsmiths, made repairs as far as the house of the temple servants and the merchants, opposite the Parade Gate, and as far as the upper room at the corner. And between the upper room of the corner and the Sheep Gate, the goldsmiths and the merchants made repairs.

—Nehemiah 3

What Do You Need to Get the Work Done?

Once you have rallied people—yes, even your congregation—to engage in building or rebuilding community, you will need to create a bridge from this excitement and commitment to action. Please understand that the bridge between commitment and action is not a sure thing. This is the place where visionaries and planners have to come together. In order to get that work done, vision, strategy, and planning all need to be in play.

Vision always generates excitement amongst people. Especially in situations where all that people have seen is dismay and despair. When a fresh picture of what can be emerges, people get excited. They get excited because a good vision produces good news. But, beginning to put the meat on the bones of a vision is very hard work. Because when you are getting people to accomplish something bigger than themselves, the work is daunting, the details can be overwhelming, and planning can be consuming. Knowing that you are about to engage in weeks of work—hard work—can cause the enthusiasm that has been initially ignited to flicker. Therefore, breaking down the work into simple steps with assignments given is paramount to achieving the vision. Keeping things easy, obvious, and strategic is good ministry practice. Failure to do this can make a short-term project a long-term burden.

I remember when we partnered with the Jewish Community Development Corporation in DC known as YACHAD, which in Hebrew means "together." We came together to transform our old, rundown church parsonage into a transitional house for families moving from homelessness to permanent residency. The project was touted as "Christmas in April," or in the Hebrew vernacular, "Succot in April."

Members of YACHAD, which encompassed members of synagogues across the city and surrounding Maryland suburbs, joined with Emory members during April of that year to make this great project a reality. The problem, however, was that after a month of work, it was quite clear that much more labor would be needed. And because there was not a clear strategy for getting the project to the finish line, soon there was a struggle to identify workers. What was originally a one-month project took the bulk of a year to complete. At one point, there were only three faithful souls working on the home, when earlier, there had been as many as fifty. The vision was strong, but the strategy was weak. We finished the project, had a wonderful ribbon cutting, but it sure did take a long time!

In my estimation, most people are visionaries, planners, or doers. Rarely do you find people who are all three. At best, visionaries are doers, and planners can be doers, but rarely do you find a visionary planner. With this reality, it becomes incumbent upon leadership to identify who they are and then build a strong team in order to create the bridge and get to work. How do you do this? The following steps can help:

1. Match passions and skills with needs. Usually the bridge building is invisible. Just like in the Nehemiah text, we see people ready to roll up their sleeves at the end of chapter 2, and then working on their assigned jobs in chapter 3. Missing in the narrative is the blueprint and action plan that undergirds the work. Nehemiah assigns some teams to particular gates and other teams to sections of the wall. From the ease in which people work in the story, we can assume that Nehemiah has put people in the right roles given their giftedness. This includes knowing people's passions—who has a passion for one thing and who has a passion for another. This also includes knowing people's skills and knowing which skills are needed where. Included in this as well is a contingency plan when changes and adjustments need to be made. We can make this assumption, reading Nehemiah's story. But we cannot make this assumption with most of our congregations. Most of our congregations are consumed with putting people's names in slots that need to be filled, rather than identifying skills and giftedness and putting them into play in an area that will matter.

Behind the scenes, it is obvious that Nehemiah and the people have taken detailed steps to make sure that vision, strategy, and planning are connected. All of this assessment and planning must have taken place between chapters 2 and 3. Because when we hit chapter 3, people with a mind to work are very busy at work!

What strikes me first when I start reading chapter 3 is that Nehemiah is silent. We just see the people working. He isn't barking out orders or micromanaging. In fact, he doesn't say a word the entire chapter. When you plan and organize the labor and then set people free to do the work, people's passions, gifts, and skills will automatically engage them in the work.

Bonnie Nicholas runs a comprehensive ministry to homeless people in her congregation in Washington, DC. She's been doing so for the last ten years. She is so committed to this, and the skills she has are so well positioned, that no one has to tell Bonnie to get to work or to do the work. Bonnie is up working before anyone else. This is what happens when people are properly positioned in the work of the body.

2. Encourage teamwork. The next thing you see in the text is teamwork, people working next to people. What becomes clear in community engagement is that it's not about one person. It is about teamwork. In December of 2013, Jameis Winston, the starting quarterback for Florida State University, won the Heisman trophy, the annual award given to the nation's best collegiate football player. Winston, instead of gloating over the trophy and his own personal accolades, took the trophy back to Florida State and used his award to motivate his teammates to win a national title. Almost a month later, it took teamwork for Florida State to overcome a twenty-one–three deficit and win the title. With one minute and fifteen seconds left to go in the game against Auburn, during the final drive, here's what Winston said in the huddle: "I said, guys, we didn't come here for no reason. I said, guys, this is ours, man. . . . And like I've been saying, we control our own destiny. And those men looked me in my eye and they said, 'We got this, Jameis.' And I said . . . 'Are you strong?' They said, 'I'm strong if you strong.' I said, 'We strong, then'" (DJ Byrnes, "Jameis Winston's Post-BCS Title Speech Was Amazing," *Eleven Warriors* [blog], January 7, 2014, www.elevenwarriors.com/2014/01/32028/jameis -winstons-post-bcs-title-speech-was-amazing).

No one person can rebuild an entire community; no one congregation can do it, either. There must be teamwork between congregation and community, everyone finding their passions, skills, and abilities and allowing them to be positioned where they are needed the most.

3. Keep traffic flowing. The other distinct characteristic in the text that relates to getting people to work is that each person knows his or her role, stays in his or her lane, and does his or her job with an eye toward the greater good. Door repairers knew who they were; door hangers knew who they were; those responsible for installing bolts and bars knew who they were; the roofers knew who they were. We don't see people trying to critique or tell someone else how to do his or her job. Nor do we see people trying to do what they are not skilled to do. This is vitally important because often people do something they like to do but aren't called or gifted to do. Or they aren't working but instead telling someone else how to do his or her job. This creates traffic jams, resentment, and confusion. It also makes work inefficient or come to a standstill because of the frustration generated.

I remember once seeking to engage the director of a neighborhood school in one of our congregational/community projects. She had great passion and giftedness for the project we were seeking to get done. However, she would not participate in the project because of her frustration with the politics that were taking place in our congregation at that time. In fact, she knew the lines of power in my congregation better than I did. It wasn't until several years later when we undertook a similar project that the director said yes because she saw that we had gotten people out of the way and opened the door for constructive work to be accomplished.

4. Allow people to work in areas of self-interest. Still another piece in getting people to work is having them work in their areas of self-interest. For example, in the text we see Jedaiah, son of Harumaph, rebuild across from his own house. Once you've identified people's self-interests in the inspection, you need to place them in roles where their self-interests can be maximized.

People show more passion and are willing to work much harder when what matters to them is a part of the tasks that they are doing. You will find people losing interest and motivation when they see no connection between their tasks and their self-interests. For example, in my work as co-chair of the Washington Interfaith Network (WIN), a fifty-member church/synagogue/mosque/labor union/social justice organization in DC, I noticed a tendency of churches after a few years of organizing across the city. It became very apparent that certain congregations gained strength or lost interest in a project depending on whether that project was in the neighborhood in which their congregation was located. In fact, recognizing this reality moved the network to encourage churches to identify projects in their neighborhoods that they would be committed to working on. When that happened, the organization grew stronger and broader. More and more community engagement work was done and projects were completed.

5. Let everyone get his or her hands dirty. A final piece to getting people to work is putting everyone to work regardless of social status. In the text, not only do you find families working next to families, but also you find mayors working next to artisans, you find priests working next to temple support staff. You find rich working next to poor. You find every class system within the community working together for the common good. When the vision is of God, everyone—regardless of race, class, gender, sexual orientation, or ethnicity—will join in and work. The most effective congregations are congregations that are multigenerational, socioeconomically diverse, and open to anyone serving in positions of leadership.

There are a number of churches across our district that have youth working next to adults to ensure ministry happens—rather than just relegating youth to the nursery. We see intergenerational teams in outreach ministries, in worship teams, and across the life of the church. In many places young people need community service hours to graduate; our churches become a great training and opportunity ground.

A great picture of these five points working in tandem can be seen in the task of the Washington Interfaith Network (WIN) to build a critical mass of solid, affordable housing for households earning between $20,000 to $60,000 per year. Ironically, we called this effort the WIN/Nehemiah Housing Project. Those who know anything about Washington, DC, know that people earning salaries in this range are either classified as the working poor or low-income wage earners. The vision came because many people in the congregations and the communities from the network were being displaced or threatened with having to move because of the rising costs of housing. So the vision was cast and people across the city from all walks of life got excited. In community rallies held to gain commitment, there were a thousand or more people representing multiple races, classes, and professions gathered in our churches at one time. In fact, Marion Barry, the mayor of Washington at that time, commented to me and a group of WIN leaders in the midst of the excitement that he'd never seen anything like it before in all his years of governing.

That was the vision casting, but the bridge needed to be built. Much planning, prayer, political leveraging, and grace is required from private institutions in order to build a critical mass of housing for people who don't have much money to pay for their residences. The network had to find a large plot of land in a city with very few vacant lots of any size. In addition, politicians needed to be persuaded to set aside huge amounts of government subsidies to significantly lower the development costs of the project so that the monthly mortgages offered to residents would be low. This is no small feat as most government subsidies are reserved for big-time developers who expect to receive a sizeable development fee for their building efforts. Furthermore, we needed to find developers who had a heart for helping the people of a lower class. And also we needed to organize the communities surrounding the land where these homes could be built in a way that assured them that the housing we were building was topflight and that the people living in them would be good neighbors. Too many people suffer from the NIMBY (Not In My Back Yard) syndrome. And too many people have an incorrect, unfair, negative perception of low-income and working-poor people. Finding the place to build these homes was a huge challenge.

To build the bridge and get to work, we began to break down our network and give assignments to people based on giftedness, self-interest, and passion for seeing low-income families own their own homes. Some of us spent all of our time convincing politicians that this was the right thing and galvanizing support from private institutions. Others devoted energies to laying out the financial plan for such a project. Still others of us did the 1:1 relational building in the targeted communities where the housing would be built and with potential homebuyers. And others simply came to rallies designed to influence politicians to take a stand for good.

It is important to realize that once you get people to work, you need to constantly and consistently encourage the work to continue. It isn't an overnight deal. While it took Nehemiah and the people of Jerusalem fifty-two days to complete the rebuilding of walls and gates, depending on your project it may take you fifty-two months to complete the project. The WIN/Nehemiah Housing Project took eight years from the conception of the vision to the grand opening of the building. Because people from multiple congregations not only had a mind to work but also got to work, there are 150 families living in affordable housing in southeast Washington who are rejoicing *every* day. What was once thought to be impossible, God, through a whole lot of folks, made possible.

What do you need to get the work done?

Personal: What is needed to get the work done? Where do you fit?

Small Group: Discuss where each person is positioned to get the work done. Are there any steps that need to be taken so that everyone is engaged? If your congregation is in the process of getting the work done, how is your small group participating? Open prayer time with praise reports and continued needs from previous weeks (prayer, being all-in, risk taking, mission field, gaining commitment), adding to it prayers for getting the work done.

Leadership Team and Congregation: Assess where your congregation is in the organization process.

How are we helping match our people's passions and skills with needs to get the work done? What's working? What ideas do we have for improvement?

How do we encourage teamwork? What's working? Which ministries are team based? What ideas do we have for improvement?

Does each person know his or her role, line of authority, and how his or her tasks are connected to the greater work? Where is traffic flowing well? What needs to be done in the areas that aren't flowing well?

How are we allowing people to join in the work in the areas of their self-interest? What are some ideas for improvement?

How are we letting everyone (children, youth, men, women, marrieds, singles, residents) get his or her hands dirty? What can we do to engage everyone in the work?

> ## Tip
>
> If your congregation has been struggling to fill slots for committees, this could feel like a daunting checklist of questions. The first thing to recognize is that we are talking about intentionally mobilizing people to team together to make a difference in the neighborhood/community. This is a task that should include people who are in the community and aren't yet in the congregation (identified through your Relational 1:1 Campaign). It usually doesn't require specialized skill sets or formal membership. But it does require focused, disciplined attention to these five areas listed above without a bias toward the people who are typically in formal leadership positions.

Step 8

Expect Opposition

Whenever a group of people commits itself to the common good—fully engaged in bringing hope to the vulnerable and defenseless—you can expect some people to ridicule and others not to participate. It is critical to keep your attention on those who are engaged and not be distracted by others.

But when Sanballat the Horonite, Tobiah the Ammonite official, and Geshem the Arab heard about it, they mocked and made fun of us. "What are you doing?" they asked. "Are you rebelling against the king?" ...
Next to them the people from Tekoa made repairs, but their officials wouldn't help with the work of their supervisors....
When Sanballat heard that we were building the wall, he became angry and raged. He mocked the Jews, saying in the presence of his associates and the army of Samaria: "What are those feeble Jews doing? Will they restore things themselves? Will they offer sacrifices? Will they

finish it in a day? Will they revive the stones from the piles of rubble, even though they are burned?"
Tobiah the Ammonite, who was beside him, added: "If even a fox climbs on whatever they build, their wall of stones will crumble."
Listen, God; we are despised! Turn their insults to us back on their heads and make them like plunder in a captive land. Don't forgive their iniquity or blot out their sins from your sight. They have thrown insults at the builders!
We continued to build the wall. All of it was joined together, and it reached half of its intended height because the people were eager to work. But when Sanballat, Tobiah, the Arabs, the Ammonites, and the people of Ashdod heard that the work on the walls was progressing and the gaps were being closed, they were very angry. They plotted together to come and fight against Jerusalem and to create a disturbance in it. So we prayed to our God and set a guard as protection against them day and night. . . .
Now when Sanballat, Tobiah, Geshem the Arab, and the rest of our enemies heard that I had rebuilt the wall and that there were no gaps left in it (although I hadn't yet hung the doors in the gates), Sanballat and Geshem sent me this message: "Come, let's meet together in one of the villages in the plain of Ono."
But they wanted to harm me, so I sent messengers to tell them, "I'm doing important work, so I can't come down. Why should the work stop while I leave it to come down to you?"
—Nehemiah 2:19; 3:5; 4:1-9; 6:1-3

How Do You Turn Opposition into Opportunity?

What I learned firsthand in co-leading the organizing of the WIN/Nehemiah Housing Project and now co-leading our congregation and community development organization's Beacon Center Project is that the greater the vision, the more the opposition. Or as someone once said, "With every new level, there's a new devil." When you seek to mend hearts and reengage communities for the better, all for the kingdom of God, you must expect opposition. Visions of God always come to pass, but in coming to fruition, they travel through great adversity. As Kirbyjon Caldwell puts it:

> Vision is the outcome, the destination, the realization of God's preferred future.... If the Calling is the path, the Vision is the destination.... A vision *stretches* reality; it's not a quick and easy fix. It's a mountain that rises up in your line of sight, at first foreboding, seemingly impossible. But the closer you get, the more attainable it becomes—if you can persevere in the face of the negative forces that are going to rise up against you. (Kirbyjon H. Caldwell and Mark Seal, *Be in It to Win It: A Roadmap to Spiritual, Emotional, and Financial Wholeness* [New York: Touchstone Faith, 2007], 127)

But don't let opposition distract you. In fact, opposition is often a sign that you are heading in the right direction. Both Moses and Joshua faced great opposition leading their congregations to the promised land. Jesus himself faced opposition all the way to a violent crucifixion but joyous resurrection. When you are seeking to bind up the brokenhearted, opposition is surely going to find you. How you handle it will determine whether you achieve success in engaging your community or fall short of reaching God's dreams.

Throughout Nehemiah's quest to rebuild the walls of Jerusalem, opposition of all types arose. When you are on your own quest, you will likewise experience all types of barriers. Some of them will be in your mind only; others will come from the anger, attitudes, and behaviors of others. Some will come in the form of mocking; still others will come from deception, trickery, and very real threat. But you must not let opposition distract you from pursuing what God broke your heart to do. The less you allow yourself to get distracted by the opposition, the more you will find God being victorious for you and those you serve in the end.

From the time that Nehemiah's heart broke, he faced six types of opposition:

1. Mental opposition. His first opposition was mental as he struggled to figure out how to get from Babylonian captivity to Jerusalem to rebuild the walls. Remember, he was in captivity and he was one thousand miles from home. His heart broke and his mind said it was impossible to do anything about it. So many people let "impossibility" trap them or even stop them from dreaming big dreams, let alone going after them. But when these mental games of opposition seek to paralyze you, remember what Nehemiah does. He fasts and prays to the God of heaven, asking that the will of God be fulfilled. And in every situation, God answers Nehemiah's prayer. The spiritual disciplines are God's pathway of moving us from anguish to anticipation. Prayer is the great vehicle for overcoming opposition. Nehemiah stays in prayer throughout his journey.

What amazes me about the churches that I visit are the number of congregations that don't pay any real attention to the development of the practice of spiritual disciplines in their people. Even though a congregation may include prayer in its worship services, the real examination of the power of prayer is missing. The spiritual disciplines aren't being taught, preached, or modeled. What serves as a powerful resource for us to live the Christian life is often being ignored by the very body that is to promote it—the church. One thing is for certain, the church doesn't need to be its own opposition!

2. Perceived opposition. Nehemiah knew that King Artaxerxes was his only way home and Nehemiah worried and won-
dered about how he was going to convince the king to let him go
back home. Again, he turned to the vehicle of prayer for an answer.
And God, through his grace, made a way. Oftentimes we do not
move forward with God-given visions to build or rebuild community because we perceive that change is not possible. Oftentimes
our congregations do not move forward because our congregations
are trapped in a "we've never done this before" or "we don't know
how to do this" mentality that stirs up worry. Still other perceived
opposition can come when we adopt the perceptions of others.

As my congregation has pressed forward to build the Beacon
Center, one of the constant refrains that we hear from those who
are against our effort and even those excited about it but doubt-
ful or concerned about how it is going to happen is, "Wow, this
surely is an ambitious project." *Ambitious project* has become code
for "we don't see how you are going to do it." Another comment
made is that our project is too "big." *Big* becomes a code word
for "it is too much for you to do" or "it's just not possible." And
some of these comments are made by people who haven't dealt
with a project that is of the scope and magnitude of the Beacon
Center. When this type of opposition arose, we went back to God
and asked: Is it too big? Is it too much? Do you want us to scale
back? I even asked God to shut it down if it was too much for us
to handle. But at every turn, God made it clear through events,
experiences, and an inner assurance that we needed to move forward. What God wants to come to pass, God will bring to pass.
What God wants to shut down, will be shut down. Our role is to
discern God's will and move forward accordingly.

Perception is one of the most dangerous of all oppositions because for many, perception is reality. They can't distinguish what they see or believe from what is real, so what they see or believe becomes what is real for them. In the same manner, perception is dangerous because it has the potential of limiting what one believes God can do. Our scriptures tell us that God can do abundantly more than we can ever ask or think. And yet our perceptions can put a lid on God. Our scriptures tell us that all things are possible with God, yet our perceptions can give the impression that there are certain things that are impossible. And so we must overcome perceived opposition by constantly praying and discerning that our thoughts, minds, and deeds are in line with God's will. And we must have faith—believing and trusting God even through some things we've never seen nor understand nor even imagine. Here the Hebrew writer encourages us: "Faith is the reality of what we hope for, the proof of what we don't see" (Hebrews 11:1).

3. Political opposition. Nehemiah experienced political opposition from the benefactors of Jerusalem's demise. In chapter 2, we are introduced to Sanballat and Tobiah, two political officials who would give Nehemiah the blues all the way up until Nehemiah and the people of Jerusalem finished the work. There are some people, I believe, who the adversary assigns to you to give you trouble. To oppose you. To make your journey toward rebuilding miserable. And there are some people who the adversary assigns to you to keep you on your knees, praying to God for direction and to maintain focus.

Depending upon the community engagement that you and your congregation are involved in, these people could hold political office or they could simply be opposed to you because they are benefiting from the current situation and fear your initiative will cause them to lose power or advantage—or both! I remember a political official in the District of Columbia who was opposed to one of our building projects simply because she had already manipulated the system so that her nephew's project would benefit. This kind of opposition has to be handled carefully. You must—as the scripture says—be wise as a serpent and harmless as a dove with these individuals. You must keep them close while not divulging anything to them or allowing them to impede your progress. That, and prayer, is how you overcome this type of opposition.

4. Dismissive opposition. Once Nehemiah had gained the commitment of the people of Israel to rebuild, Sanballat and Tobiah and a third political official named Geshem begin to laugh and mock Nehemiah and his community's efforts to reestablish the walls of Jerusalem. Through political posturing and gamesmanship, these leaders sought to minimize or trivialize the project in an attempt to cause people who were committed to be discouraged or less enthusiastic about the project. They asked, "Are you rebelling against the king?" Instead of answering their questions, Nehemiah pointed to the King of all—God—as the one leading their community engagement efforts. Because of that, God would grant them success. In doing so, Nehemiah raised the game.

As long as you know it is God leading you, whatever opposition God brings you to, God will bring you through. In pursuing the Beacon Center project, there were a couple of political officials who laughed at us. They mocked our project. They characterized it as being incompetent and used their position to discourage us from moving forward. Instead of turning to anger, we turned to God. And God, in turn, moved us to begin building relationships with the very people who mocked us. One person has since found a new job. The other has become one of our greatest allies in seeing that our project gets done. If you don't allow the dismissive opposition of others to denigrate you, God can turn what looks bleak into a blessing.

5. Apathy. In Nehemiah 3:5 we read of a group of nobles who simply would not work with their master to rebuild the walls and refused to get their hands dirty with this kind of work. There are some folks who show up and give the impression they are onboard, but then refuse to lift a finger. They show an external support for you, but when the deal goes down, they are content to watch. This kind of opposition can be extremely discouraging and distracting. Their apathy is almost like poison because these are people who you think are in the battle with you. Like you may have, I have known many people who have expressed excitement for our heart-mending efforts in community. They have enthusiasm for what we are trying to do and convey sheer joy for the step-by-step accomplishments they see God bringing to pass. Yet they refuse to get dirty when it is time to work. Some of these individuals are supposed to be leaders within our congregation! Like the nobles in the Nehemiah text, people see them as leaders, people think they are leaders, and people even follow them only to discover that when it is time to do something, these leaders are like cotton candy—they are enticing from the outside but lack substance on the inside. But again, Nehemiah and the people refuse to let this type of opposition stand in their way. In fact, no one says a word and the people just keep working.

Perhaps you find yourself right now in a situation where apathy is discouraging or frustrating you. If so, pour your energy into the coalition of willing workers, realizing that it is unlikely that you will get 100 percent participation but knowing that where two or three are gathered, God is in the midst. God always has enough people with you to accomplish God's mission.

6. Real opposition. From chapter 4 all the way to the completion of the wall in chapter 6, Nehemiah and his people face real opposition. There are violent threats to get them to stop working, which leaves Nehemiah's workers carrying a tool in one hand and a weapon in the other. And there are political and socioeconomic threats, where local officials use their clout to undermine the residents of Jerusalem and unjustly place them in a system of economic suppression. When you, your congregation, and community are all-in to see that righteousness, justice, and wholeness are achieved for all, you will find that the stakes to this game can be very high. And some very real threats can come.

I recall a community action that I was a part of, seeking to gain government support for an affordable housing project. I was one of the leaders who was scheduled to go meet with the decision maker to persuade her to sign a document of approval, while at the same time two hundred protestors were singing church hymns out in front of her office to provide external pressure. The night before the rally, I received a call from a pastor who was the friend of a friend close to the decision maker. He said to me: "Tell Joe that if I were him, I wouldn't show up tomorrow. If he knew what was good for him, he'd stay home from the rally." When major dollars are on the line, threats like this are not to be taken lightly. You never know what somebody is up to. But, in spite of the threat, I went anyhow and instead of going to the decision maker's office, I led the two hundred in praying and singing outside! That day—thanks be to God—we got the support needed to go forward with the project. The Apostle Paul reminds us through a young Timothy that God did not give us a spirit of fear, but a spirit of power, love, and a sound mind.

In congregations across the country, there needs to be more of a spirit of power, love, and a sound mind. Because without this spirit, the opposition to build or rebuild community often happens from within. It can come from people who have worked hard to keep their churches open, let alone functioning, in lean times. Or it can come from people who are anxious in the midst of seasons of transition.

This type of opposition is another example of real opposition. It is real because there's the threat of people leaving the church due to disagreements around the direction the church is taking. If you are the pastor, it is critical that you love people throughout the process and keep praying with them for God to create unity and a pathway forward. If you are not the pastor and you have a mind to work toward rebuilding, it is helpful to keep the pastor encouraged and undergirded in prayer. Furthermore, some opposition will happen because those who oppose think energy needs to be spent caring for needs inside the congregation. It is essential that time is given for holy conferencing because it is an opportunity for solutions to be improved, for healing to come, and for teaching to happen.

When you engage community like Nehemiah did, you and your congregation must expect opposition. But if, like Nehemiah and the congregation of Jerusalem, you refuse to stop working and stay focused on the mission at hand and the people who are working to rebuild, you will find that God is the God who will never leave you or forsake you. When you engage with God— and encourage others to do the same—God will engage with you and do marvelous and wonderful things that perhaps you never thought were possible.

Who do you need to ignore? What seeds of discord do you need to be mindful of? What opposition do you need to turn into opportunity?

Personal: As an individual, who are the people you need to ignore? What seeds of discord do you see around you that you know in your gut you need to be mindful of?

Small Group: Discuss each type of opposition and ask people in the group to share what types they are experiencing. Open prayer time with praise reports and continued needs from previous weeks (prayer, being all-in, risk taking, mission field, gaining commitment, organizing the work), adding to it prayers for overcoming the specific instances of opposition named in the group.

Leadership Team and Congregation: Determine your corporate plan for addressing the type of opposition that is currently active and seeking to block God's work.

- Mental opposition

- Perceived opposition

- Political opposition

- Dismissive opposition

- Apathy

- Real opposition

> ## → Tip ←
>
> When opposition comes, the biggest issue for most people is staying emotionally neutral. For some, opposition is an indicator to fight, for others it is to run away or back down. It is critical that a congregation facing opposition of any kind enter into a season of prayer and fasting. Not only will this help strengthen the sense of peace in the midst of turmoil, it focuses people on the fact that this is really God's battle.

Step 9

Build Momentum

T o get to the finish line you've got to become friends with "Big Mo." Big Mo, in case you haven't met him or her, is momentum. If you want to experience victory, you had better pay attention to momentum and do all you can to build it from the start of your heartbreak to its resolution.

So I took up a position in the lowest parts of the space behind the wall in an open area. Then I stationed the people by families, and they had their swords, spears, and bows. After reviewing this, I stood up and said to the officials, the officers, and the rest of the people, "Don't be afraid of them! Remember that the Lord is great and awesome! Fight for your families, your sons, your daughters, your wives, and your houses!" Then our enemies heard that we had found out and that God had spoiled their plans. So we all returned to doing our own work on the wall. . . . Now when Sanballat, Tobiah, Geshem the Arab, and the rest of our enemies heard that I had rebuilt the wall and that there were no gaps left in it (although I hadn't yet hung the doors in the gates), Sanballat

and Geshem sent me this message: "Come, let's meet together in one of the villages in the plain of Ono."
But they wanted to harm me, so I sent messengers to tell them, "I'm doing important work, so I can't come down. Why should the work stop while I leave it to come down to you?"
They sent me a message like this four times, and every time I gave them a similar reply....
All of them were trying to make us afraid, saying, "They will be discouraged, and the work won't get finished." But now, God, strengthen me!...
So the wall was finished on the twenty-fifth day of the month of Elul. It took fifty-two days.
—Nehemiah 4:13-15; 6:1-4, 9, 15

How Are You Starting, Building, and Protecting Momentum?

Surely, if memory serves me correctly, my physics professor in high school defined *momentum* as the quantity of motion of a moving body measured as a product of its mass and velocity. Furthermore, the professor said that momentum is the impetus gained by a moving object. Simply put, when energy is moving for the positive, great things happen. When energy is working against you, it can feel as if you are climbing uphill or getting run over.

So it is with congregations and communities seeking to build and rebuild walls that have been torn down or gates that have been burned. And people have been left vulnerable and defenseless to external forces that seek to steal joy and snuff out life.

When momentum is on your side, vibrant communities will

be established. When momentum is working against you, trouble and disgrace will be the order of the day. The key to any restoration effort is to build momentum and keep it at least until the desired community outcome is accomplished.

Momentum starts for Nehemiah and the people of Jerusalem when together they decide to rise up and restore Jerusalem. You know when momentum has started because opposition begins to arise. However, when momentum is stronger than opposition, things move forward. In a football game, you can tell when momentum starts for one team. What typically happens is that one of the teams catches a break and then begins to dominate the line of scrimmage. And whenever one team dominates over another on the line of scrimmage, movement happens. Either an offense scores points or a defense forces a punt.

Our task as learners and followers of Jesus Christ is to create momentum for the kingdom of God. Such it is for Nehemiah and the people of Jerusalem. They rise up, have a mind to work, and immediately get to work. Individuals and families, priests and politicians, engineers and architects, men and women, boys and girls start working on the restoration movement. Chapter 3 gives us a picture of momentum rolling.

However, there are some very distinct, important, and critical steps necessary for congregations and communities to keep momentum moving in the process of restoration.

1. Remember whose work you are doing. Key to building momentum for God-ordained purposes is remembering that you are doing this work for God more than for anyone else. It is important to keep that perspective because folks will challenge you when they see you doing great things for God. And it will be very easy for you to be discouraged. Early on in my community devel-

opment experiences, I remember having the opportunity to se-
cure two crack houses next to our church. The momentum behind
us securing these properties and renovating them for low-income
families was huge. From bankers to block captains, many affirmed
and supported our efforts. However, one of the key politicians in
our community was not for us. And she put every roadblock in our
way to thwart our efforts. And she did so with success.

We could have stopped there and allowed the opposition to
defeat us, but instead we paused to remember that we were doing God's work and that if God didn't want us to have that site
to build housing, God had another site. Soon thereafter, a house
down the street from us became vacant. We bought it against even
more opposition. And over the last fifteen years, it has served as
a residence for subsidized senior housing and as the offices for
our 501c3. You've got to keep remembering whose work you are
doing. And you've got to let God deal with the mockery, attacks,
and opposition through prayer. Nehemiah never stopped working
while he was praying. Stay focused on God. Talk to God at every
juncture you need to, and don't be afraid.

2. Be enthusiastic. We are told that early on half the wall was
completed because the people worked with enthusiasm (4:6). They
were so excited by Nehemiah's vision that they were consumed with
seeing it come to pass. Enthusiasm comes from the Greek word
enthousiasmos, which means "to be possessed by God" so that we can
inspire others for God. It is a necessary attribute for change agents
seeking to rebuild neighborhoods and congregations. Sometimes
in the deep, tedious, and demanding work of constructing new
dreams and fresh aspirations, you need some cheerleaders around
you. Not persons with pom-poms, but you need people who can
speak a word of inspiration in your life to keep you going, and you
need to be able to do the same for others. Positioning yourself for

God to possess you is essential. When you work with enthusiasm, it is contagious and provides spirit fuel to keep the momentum going.

I'm finding that post-Pentecostal Peters and Paulas, if you don't mind me using that phrase, have great power to inspire and do so boldly. They have had an in-filling of the Holy Spirit, know why they are doing what they are doing, and seek to encourage and inspire others to do the same. On the other hand, pre-Pentecostal Peters and Paulas give up quickly when things get hot in the kitchen. Work gets done when people do things with enthusiasm.

3. Create special teams. I had the privilege of playing basketball while matriculating as a student in college. I played for three outstanding coaches: Gary Williams, who won a National Championship with the University of Maryland; Ed Tapscott, who has served as a top level executive for several NBA teams and even coached the Washington Wizards for a year; and Fran Dunphy, who has led teams at the University of Pennsylvania and Temple University to multiple NCAA appearances. Having played and coached for these three leaders, I learned the value and importance of creating special teams.

Most people think that special teams are reserved for football, only involving kick-off, punt, and field goal teams. But the reality is that basketball teams have multiple special teams. There are teams established to give the starters a rest. There are press teams designed to apply a unique type of pressure on the opponent during particular times of the game. There are even teams constructed for special situations in the game like the last two minutes of a game. My coaches were expert strategists for having substitution patterns that placed specialized teams on the floor to address almost every game situation.

Such it is for Nehemiah and the people of Israel. In order to maintain and grow momentum against increasingly hostile opposition, they have to establish special teams. At one point, they need a team to stand guard day and night to protect themselves. At another point, they need a team of builders who can carry a weapon in one hand and a construction tool in the other. At still another point, Nehemiah establishes a special team that scouts for trouble in order to give a warning of impending opposition. Without these special teams, not only would Nehemiah not be able to maintain momentum, but also the walls and gates of Jerusalem would never be restored.

If you fail to construct such special teams, you don't have a chance in seeing the work of community restoration come to completion. Special teams enable us to increase our capacity for work. To keep building momentum, you must constantly keep your eyes open for who around you can come help finish the work. Nehemiah is constantly recruiting, repositioning, and encouraging people to work. He has to. Depending on the size and complexity of the call or the heartbreak you have to resolve, you may find yourself needing to do the same.

4. Nip complaints in the bud. Complaining and building momentum are at the opposite sides of the restoration spectrum. If you are going to keep momentum going as your congregation and community seeks to revitalize themselves, then you must master the art of nipping complaints in the bud. I learned this early in my life from my dad. I remember graduating from college and seeking to find employment. I was young but found a great-paying job that I knew was mine. In fact, the office that was going to hire me all but offered me the job before I left the interview. However, when I got home, I received a phone call from the director who asked me if I had government status. I asked what that was. She said that in order for them to be able to hire me, I had to show that I had worked full-time for one year in the government. I asked her how I could do that; I'd been in school full-time. While I had worked part-time government jobs, I hadn't worked one job for a full year. Subsequently, I was unable to be hired for that job.

Needless to say, I was angry. I was out of school, ready to go, and had dollar signs swirling in my head. I complained for days about how unfair the year requirement was. The next day I woke up complaining. My father pulled me aside and said, "Son, don't cry too loud. Someone is dying to be in your shoes." When I looked around and saw what I had been able to accomplish, and the fact that I had food to eat, a place to lay my head, and clothes to wear, I immediately stopped whining. My dad had nipped the complaint in the bud.

It is natural for people to complain. When things aren't going right or fair or going the way we think they should, the easiest thing to do is complain. We whine, we fuss, we get frustrated, and suddenly the enthusiasm and energy once devoted to a positive cause suddenly causes us to slow down, wind down, and get tired. In other situations, where we simply find ourselves on the short end of injustice and discover that systems have been set up to keep us marginalized, our complaints are valid ones, but if they are not channeled in healthy, transformative ways, they can also impede our progress.

Nehemiah has to nip multiple instances of complaining in the bud. In chapter 4, he has to address the complaints of those working in the midst of fierce opposition and who are getting tired. He has to learn how to encourage them and devise strategies for giving them rest while keeping the rebuilding going. One of those strategies is assigning people to special teams. Sometimes just changing the nature of the work is enough to get people re-energized. This is a very important step for Nehemiah to take because oftentimes leaders will seek to ignore or trivialize complaints. We will act like it is no big deal or that people are just running off at the mouth. But we can't have this attitude. If the complaint is thematic and consistent, then no matter how small it may appear, a solution is needed. The longer it takes to implement a solution, the bigger the issue will become and the more momentum will be lost.

In chapter 5, there is a different set of complaints. There are people who don't have enough food to survive, there are others who have mortgaged their property to get food, and there are others who are subjected to unfair taxes; there is a community subject to a system of bondage. When Nehemiah hears this, he becomes very angry. He challenges the officials who are overseeing this system and calls them into account. Congregations and communities need to constantly equip themselves in the art of civic engagement and power analysis. So often people in our congregations and communities do not understand the basic tenets of how communities work. We need to understand that every community has a private, governmental, and public sector. How these three sectors engage with one another often determines whether segments of the community are dealt with justly.

Nehemiah understands the need for this civic engagement. Far too often leaders and congregations are so focused on getting our particular project done that we ignore very real need happening around us in our communities. And we fail to take time to address it. In the midst of restoring Jerusalem, Nehemiah pauses and begins to organize those on the margins so that the system of oppression will come to an end. Toward that end, Nehemiah calls a public meeting to demand that these unfair practices amongst the poor stop and to offer a plan for how fair treatment of all with regards to food and money can be established. Because he does this the priests, nobles, officials, and the entire assembly change their system and begin treating people fairly. Nehemiah then devotes himself and the people to returning to the wall and finishing the work. The fact of the matter is that if Nehemiah had not stopped to address this pressing issue within his community, the wall wouldn't have been able to be completed. He effectively nips complaints in the bud.

5. Hold people accountable—even yourself. Before moving forward, another word needs to be spoken about accountability. In most congregations the word *accountability* is often viewed as a curse word. Not only do we not like to use it, but also when it is used, it is considered offensive. Yet, it is the very thing that congregations need to keep work going and to get work done. And it is one of the very critical aspects that unite a community to a congregation in restoration work.

Many people stay away from congregations because leaders will not hold other leaders accountable and a spirit of accountability is absent from the fellowship.

Recently, a minister who is a member of our congregation but who now lives on the west coast came back to us to lead a men's summit. He spoke powerfully about the need to be accountable as church leaders. In his presentation, he spoke about his past years as a gang member in San Francisco. He articulated elegantly and powerfully about the demands and expectations of being a member of a street gang. He went into great detail about the blessings and the penalties related to accountability or the lack thereof. This was all before he had given his life to Christ and turned his life around. He said that when he left the gang and got to the church, he really struggled. He still struggles to this day, because he was used to operating in a culture with strong accountability and that was nowhere to be found in the church. He could make a connection between basic principles shared by gangs and the church. For example, there were initiation rights, a sense of belonging, the notion and definition of membership in both. But when it came to living out membership, the church woefully lagged behind when it came to accountability. Because of this, the minister finds himself struggling to stay connected to a body that does not represent who he knows Jesus to be. All because accountability is not stressed.

The great thing about Nehemiah is that accountability is in his blood. He is accountable to God, accountable to King Artaxerxes, accountable to the people of Jerusalem, and accountable to working with all he has until the restoration of his heart is complete. In addition to holding officials accountable and changing an oppressive system, at the end of chapter 5, Nehemiah himself is appointed governor and takes upon himself the feeding of 150 officials plus visitors from other lands while asking for nothing in return.

6. Control the tempo and the message. As we have seen, Nehemiah is masterful at building momentum. Nehemiah and the people constantly keep before them whose work they are doing. They exhibit a high level of enthusiasm even in the face of oppression. Nehemiah creates special teams and recruits as many people to the cause as he can, increasing capacity as the work progresses. He nips complaints in the bud and holds people accountable—even himself. And yet another discipline he can teach us as we seek to build our own momentum is that throughout the restoration and rebuilding work that congregations and communities engage in, we must always control the tempo and the message. Because the moment you allow the opposition to control the tempo or the message, you lose ground that may not be reclaimable.

Back to my ball-playing days in college—those three coaches were masters at controlling tempo and messages. I learned a great deal from them about the importance of controlling or changing tempo in the game. At times we would press to gain momentum; at other times, we would slow the game down to keep momentum. Sometimes we would alternate tactics to keep our opponent off balance. Every time we controlled tempo, we won. Every time we relinquished tempo to our opposition, we lost momentum and sometimes even the game.

Nehemiah specializes in controlling tempo, particularly as he gets close to finishing the wall. In chapter 6, seeing that the work on the wall is almost complete, Nehemiah's greatest enemies—Sanballat, Tobiah, and Geshem, along with their buddies—put on a last-minute, full-court press to try and get Nehemiah to stop. They try to get Nehemiah off the wall by shifting the tempo and the message. On four occasions, they come with the same message and Nehemiah refuses to come down from the wall. The fifth time, they change their tactic and deliver a letter in an effort to intimidate and discourage Nehemiah and the workers. But instead of succumbing to the pressure, Nehemiah increases his determination and directly refutes the statements made. Later, his enemies try a more personal approach as Nehemiah goes to visit someone who is sick and confined to his home. But because Nehemiah remains connected to God and remembers whose work it is, he is not fooled or intimidated or discredited but continues to control both tempo and message.

As most successful coaches tell their teams, it is a sixty-minute game. You have to play until the horn sounds or the whistle blows. Every second, you have to be on. Or as Dick Motta, the former coach of the Washington Bullets (now known as the Wizards) popularized during the only NBA championship season the Bullets have had: "The opera ain't over until the fat lady sings."

7. Persist until the work is done. From the beginning of the work until the very end, there will always be moments when you will be tempted to quit. Even with momentum squarely on your side, the impulse to give up will still hover near you or around you. Nehemiah's final lesson in building momentum is to never quit but instead persist until the work is all the way done.

I remember studying for my doctor of ministry degree. I had reached a point in my studies where my workload as a pastor had gotten extremely heavy and where one of my professors was making life unnecessarily difficult in the classroom. I was ready to throw in the towel. But I remember sharing this with one of my ministerial colleagues who was in school with me. I'll never forget what she said: "Go back and examine where you are. You are probably closer to being finished than you think you are." When I stepped away from my troubles, I realized that I was just a little more than a semester away from graduating. Had I quit, I would have forfeited the vast majority of work that I had already completed and, obviously, would not have attained my degree. Persistence is critical to building momentum and finishing the work.

Nehemiah is a master of persistence. He sticks with the work through thick and thin. And even when there is pressure for him to come down from the work at the eleventh hour, he refuses, pushes his way through, and eventually celebrates the completion of the wall in just fifty-two days. What his heart had broken for months beforehand is now restored. You can only imagine the shout that breaks out when lives and a community suddenly see that God has completed through God's people what God had started. Not only is God's vision fulfilled, but Nehemiah—whose name means "the Lord has comforted"—has fulfilled his purpose as he completes the work that comforts his people.

More and more of our congregations and communities will celebrate like Nehemiah and the people of Jerusalem if we build momentum, keep momentum, and persist until the work is complete. And the community will have a far better attitude toward the church when such realities come to pass.

Build momentum and finish the work! You can do it!

Personal: How are you starting, building, or protecting momentum?

Small Group: Discuss the importance of starting, building, and protecting momentum, and identify which momentum builders are most relevant right now given the restoration project you are engaged in. Open prayer time with praise reports and continued needs from previous weeks (prayer, being all-in, risk taking, mission field, gaining commitment, organizing the work, addressing opposition), adding to it prayers for building and protecting momentum.

Leadership Team and Congregation: Assess your congregation's Big Mo then determine your corporate plan for starting, building, and protecting momentum.

Answer true or false for each statement. Then, for each false, identify a plan for making it true for your congregation.

Our congregation is very clear that we are doing God's work.

Our leaders and workers are enthusiastic—possessed and guided by God.

We create special teams periodically to respond to urgent needs and give people a change of pace.

Leaders nip complaints in the bud.

Leaders hold people—and one another—accountable.

We do a good job of controlling the tempo and the message.

We persist—we don't give up—until projects are complete.

➤ Tip ◄

If your congregation has more falses than trues in the momentum inventory above, you will need to approach creating momentum with an intentional belief and expectation that God is able. Additionally you will need to check that all key leaders—formal and informal—have a positive attitude, including YOU! Finally, seek to improve the area above that is the quickest "win" for your congregation. And be sure to celebrate it when you accomplish it.

Appendix

Relational 1:1 Campaign Example

You will need to train folks on how to do a relational 1:1 conversation and give them a chance to practice before launching the campaign. We recommend contacting your local Industrial Areas Foundation chapter or community organizing entity to help conduct this training.

What follows is an example of how we follow up this training so that all interviewers are on the same page. We have found it essential to follow up the training with a written campaign outline that provides clear expectations, timelines, and talking points.

Relational Meeting Campaign: [Insert 3-4 Week Date Range]

Leader Information Sheet

    1. Set-up and conduct at least five relational meetings.

- Try to make your first meeting with another leader who has been trained for the campaign. [Provide information about where the interactive list may be found.]

- The majority (or all) your interviews will be with someone at our church. Meet them at a safe, public place of their choosing (e.g., coffee shop, a park).

- [Explain the system of choosing and contacting folks].

- If you meet with people not on this list, you can post a message to the group or e-mail [point person's name and e-mail address] to be added to the list so we can keep track of who has had meetings.

- If you are apprehensive about initiating a meeting, check with [insert point person's name] to see if he or she is available to go with you on the first couple of interviews. The point person could do the first interview and you could observe (then you'd complete the reflection together). The second interview you would conduct and he or she would observe.

- The following three are examples of what you might say when calling or talking with someone to set up the meeting:

  1. For those on the general list:

     Hi! I'm [name] and am part of a team [insert pastor's name] has put together to discover more about our leaders and potential leaders. I got your name from [name]. I'd like to schedule a thirty- to forty-minute meeting with you to get a sense of who you are and what you are interested in and then explore how your talents and passions might intersect with needs in our community.

2. For those on the sign-up or survey list: [Example: The first Sunday of the ENGAGE series, we asked people to sign-up to learn more about how to get engaged. The remaining four Sundays of the ENGAGE series, we are encouraging people to complete an ENGAGE survey and those people are being told that someone will be contacting them. Those names will be posted to the Interviewer group by each Monday. If you sign-up to interview someone from this category, be sure to contact him or her before Friday!]

Hi! I'm [name] and am part of a team [insert pastor's name] has put together to discover more about our leaders and potential leaders. I understand that you signed up to learn more about how you might get better engaged at our church. I'd like to schedule a thirty- to forty-minute meeting with you to get a sense of who you are and what you are interested in and then explore how your talents and passions might intersect with needs in our community.

3. For those you choose in the community:

Hi! I'm [name] and am part of a team [insert pastor's name] from [insert church's name]—you know [pastor's name]—has put together to discover more about leaders and potential leaders who are invested in community transformation. I'd like to schedule a thirty- to forty-minute meeting with you to get a sense of who you are and what you are interested in and then explore how that might shape or intersect with needs in the broader community.

2. Create the story that you will share with each person you interview.

Your story needs to include why you are invested in this process, and it should set the tone for authenticity. Share something personal so those being interviewed are more comfortable taking the same risk with you.

3. Open the meeting with a reminder of the framework for the conversation and your story.

Per the outline distributed at the training, your story should be a "brief introduction of yourself and key turning points for you (where you grew up, what you care about, why you live here now, why you joined the church, what your goals are for the church, your role in that)."

You might say something like:

> *Thanks so much for making the time for this conversation. As you know, I am part of a team [insert pastor's name] has put together to discover more about our leaders and potential leaders. In the next thirty to forty minutes I'd like to get a sense of who you are and what you are interested in and then explore how your talents and passions might intersect with needs in our community.*
>
> *I'll start by letting you know a little about myself. I grew up in and around Oberlin, Ohio, and came to the DC area about sixteen years ago. I came to our church in 2007 as a part of a United Methodist research team that was seeking to learn what makes transformational congregations tick. I was so taken with the warmth, authenticity, and presence of the Holy Spirit at our church that I couldn't*

*stay away. Soon I brought my children with me
and joined the church. Over the past several years I
have been blown away by the people God has been
sending us. I have been working with various leaders and ministries to find better ways of connecting
those gifts and talents in the life of our congregation
and wider community. I think that when the right
God-sent people are operating in the right place,
God will magnify the blessing we are to the community. What brought you to our church?*

4. Be curious about what makes them tick.

• Conversationally ask "why" questions to inquire, not pry.

• Ask questions that invigorate conversation, but that don't
irritate.

• Use the outline provided in the training but make it feel
like a conversation, not an interview.

5. Thank them for the conversation and offer a potential next
step.
   The next step may not be the same for everyone:

• For church folk, you can explain how these interviews will
be used to gather information on the passions and talents
within the congregation, find common themes, and organize and engage people around those interests.

   1. Who do you know at our church that this person might
   want to get to know better?

2. Who might this person recommend you speak with next?

- For community folk their next step would be based upon their self-interest (their personal grounding for their public actions).

  1. What step might you challenge them to make based on what you learned in the interview?

6. Write down your reflections and [insert where/how you want people to share their notes].

- Please do not take notes during the meeting. *However,* you will be writing your mental notes on the reflection form immediately following the meeting.

- Use the reflection form to jot down what you learned.

- You are responsible for entering the information from the reflection cards and surveys you collect [insert where/how you want people to share their notes] no later than the end of the campaign [insert date]. We are asking you to do so, so that we don't have to interpret handwriting.

- [Tip: If you are using a web-based tool for data collection you will need to make accommodations for those who aren't comfortable with that environment.] If you don't have access to the Internet, you may give your forms to [point person] or drop your notes in the offering basket during service.

If you have questions about the campaign or what you should do, please contact [insert point person's name, phone number, and e-mail address].

CPSIA information can be obtained
at www.ICGtesting.com
Printed in the USA
LVOW13s1504060517
533463LV00008B/59/P